CHAUCER STUDIES IX

CHAUCER AND THE POEMS OF 'CH'

CHAUCER AND THE POEMS OF 'CH'

in University of Pennsylvania MS French 15

JAMES I. WIMSATT

D. S. BREWER · ROWMAN & LITTLEFIELD

First published 1982 by D. S. Brewer
240 Hills Road, Cambridge
an imprint of Boydell & Brewer Ltd, PO Box 9,
Woodbridge, Suffolk IP12 3DF
and Rowman & Littlefield Inc, 81 Adams Drive,
Totowa, New Jersey N.J. 07512, USA

British Library Cataloguing in Publication Data

Chaucer and the poems of 'Ch'.—(Chaucer studies
  ISSN 0261-9822; 9)
  1. Chaucer, Geoffrey—Authorship
  2. French poetry—to 1500
  I. Wimsatt, James I.   II. Series
  841'.1'09

  ISBN 0-85991-130-6
  US ISBN 0-8476-7200-X

C
ν

Photoset in Great Britain by
Rowland Phototypesetting Ltd, Bury St Edmunds, Suffolk
and printed by St Edmundsbury Press
Bury St Edmunds, Suffolk

Contents

Illustrations

PREFATORY NOTE

In the mid-fourteenth century the knights and poets of the London courts participated fully in the French lyric mode. Though Chaucer was deeply involved in the life of these courts, and inevitably in their poetry, many of the basic materials which relate to English participation in this poetic mode have not been brought together and made available. As a Chaucerian I find these materials of deep interest and of strong relevance to Chaucer's career as poet. This edition and study aims to make some of the most important of them generally available to Chaucer scholars. The University of Pennsylvania manuscript which I draw on here is a unique source of relevant texts; to study it is to place oneself in the midst of the French poetic world that Chaucer entered in the late 1350's.

I wish to thank the Charles Patterson Van Pelt Library of the University of Pennsylvania for permission to use their MS French 15, and to register my appreciation to Professor William Kibler of the University of Texas at Austin Department of French and Italian for his generous advice on the translation and editing of the French texts; any deficiencies in these, however, are certainly not ascribable to him. My thanks to others who gave me counsel on the MS dating and provenance is recorded in the appropriate notes. I also want to acknowledge the great assistance which Charles Mudge's groundbreaking dissertation on the MS provided me. It is unfortunate that he did not live to publish it.

James I. Wimsatt
Austin, Texas
April 10, 1982

1. *University of Pennsylvania MS French 15, f.77v, showing rubrics of three ballades, with 'Ch' inserted in a different hand beside and beneath two of the rubrics (edited as Ch VII and VIII).*

PART I

The Poems of 'Ch'

INTRODUCTION

Among the 310 French lyrics that make up University of Pennsylvania manuscript French 15, a late fourteenth century codex, are fifteen poems which have the initials 'Ch' neatly inserted between rubric and text. The best guess as to the significance of these initials is that they indicate authorship.[1] Since there are no obvious candidates among the French poets of the time,[2] and since it has been suggested by more than one sober authority that Chaucer began his poetic career writing French poems of the very sort that 'Ch' produced, the question arises if 'Ch' could have been Geoffrey Chaucer. A number of features of the manuscript do indeed indicate that the 'Ch' lyrics might have been composed in English court circles when Chaucer was in his first years of court service in London; that is, in the decade beginning in 1357 or a bit earlier.[3] Nevertheless, he would be a bold scholar indeed who would claim outright that 'Ch' stands for Chaucer. For while the works display a measure of wit and skill within the limitations of the fashionable forms, they are not consistently outstanding. If they bear comparison with some of Chaucer's love lyrics, they hardly show the genius of his mature narratives, and one can find in them but few specific foretokens of his English poetry.

In editing the poems, then, I do not propose to make a case for Chaucer's authorship of the works. Rather, by presenting the 'Ch' texts, together with the evidence which tends to connect them with Chaucer's circle and his time, I have the more modest purpose of suggesting more precisely than has been done what Chaucer's French poetry might have been like if one assumes that he followed the normal course of the literate young courtier of the time by writing French lyrics in the fixed forms on the subject of love. The body of fifteen poems is coherent and at the same time varied. It is representative of the time in form, subject matter, and treatment. To my knowledge there is extant no comparable set of French lyrics from the mid-fourteenth century with equivalent relevance to Chaucer.

By way of introducing the edition and translation of the fifteen poems, let us first attempt to place them in their milieu. If we postulate for the poet 'Ch' a situation such as we might for a young associate of Chaucer whose early career was like his, we may imagine something like the following. 'Ch' entered service in one of the major English courts around 1357 at the age of fourteen. Though his first language was English, he had become fluent in French so that he conversed readily in both court languages. Since by nature he was a good conversationalist as well as an apt student of languages, he soon became a regular participant in ducal and royal entertainments and excursions about England. On such occasions he often heard poetry sung and recited both by established court poets and by his less literary fellows; in theory, all courtiers 'koude songes make and well endite,' and most tried to do so. Having already found out at school that he was clever in Latin composition, 'Ch' soon tried his own skill in the fashionable modes of court verse. It was, of course, French verse, French having been the vernacular of royal court literature in England for centuries. The courtiers wrote their poetry in French, and it did not occur to a beginner like 'Ch' to do otherwise.

The poetic mode that 'Ch' learned at court, a mode that grew up in the late thirteenth and early fourteenth century, was highly artificial; it confined form and substance within narrow bounds. While the mode grew out of the Old French trouvère tradition, the flexible metrical forms of the trouvères had given way to the complex *formes fixes* of ballade, chant royal, lay, virelay, and rondeau. Each of these had its strict metrical requirements. The subject materials and their treatment were also restricted. The great, if not exclusive, subject of the lyrics was noble love. Each poem consisted of a little essay or drama on its subject, developed mainly in three ways. One way was by use of personification allegory, mainly grounded on the *Roman de la Rose*. Another was through reference to old stories: classical narratives, Bible narratives, and medieval romance. A third was by focussing on a conventional image: the fiery desire of the lover, the stony heart of the lady, the lover's final testament, and so on.

Particularized and immediate emotions of love did not supply the primary inspiration of this poetry; instead, what evoked the poems was the writers' desire to play well the court game of poetry. They did not need current, ardent love affairs; rather, they needed grammar, rhetoric, and a certain amount of reading so as to comply creatively with the game's demanding rules. They also needed something less palpable, an understanding of the aspirations of their society, since the earnest purpose inspiriting the game was that of locating in the courtiers' sensibilities their ideals of being and behavior, and of mirroring these ideals for the audience.

The poet held up the ideal for the court audience's analysis and considera-tion. The audience's response, educated and conditioned as it was by repetition of the same forms, subjects, and treatments, was inevitably intellectual in character. Hearing for the fiftieth time a lover's last testament, or a lady's lament over a traitorous lover, the auditors would certainly not be moved to tears; ironic detachment was bound to control. This freed them for impersonal admiration and criticism of the ideal as embodied in the poems: admiration of virtues such as patience, devotion, and fidelity inherent in the ideal; amused criticism of the simplicity, credulousness, and shallowness which it also entails. Contributing to the admiration would be the evidence of control and virtuousity inherent in the complex forms. Contributing to the ironic effects would be the potential discrepancy between the statements of the poems and the possible underlying intent; at various levels beneath the always decorous diction one might infer illicit passion, immoral design, and immoderate behavior.

Young 'Ch', then, did not need to find a real-life object of his affections in order to write poems for an English court, nor would he have at a French court; his audience did not concern itself with who the lady of his poems *really* was. And they did not look to him for new forms or materials. They were chiefly interested in how he handled the given form and material, and in the tact with which he presented their ideals. A consideration of his works, then, needs to take into account these audience expectations which would have governed his composition.

Ten of 'Ch's' fifteen lyrics are three-stanza ballades, four are five-stanza chants royaux, and one is a rondeau. In their particular metrics the ballades are like many composed in England and northern France from about 1340. For ballades they are quite lengthy. Eight have stanzas ten lines long, one has stanzas twelve lines long, and one eight lines long. All have the standard one or two-line refrains, and—as was usual before the work of Eustache Deschamps—they lack envoys. 'Ch's' chants royaux have nine, ten, and eleven-line stanzas very similar to the ballade strophes. They have envoys but no refrains, which again agrees with standard practice before Deschamps.[4] The rondeau has a common eight-line form. Through the fifteen poems the lines are decasyllabic (eleven syllables feminine).

The dry facts about the metrics provide some solid information about 'Ch'. In total, they suggest composition after lyric poets were no longer presumed to be musical composers (near mid-century) and before Deschamps' mature work (c.1370). The ballade stanza of ten decasyllabic lines which he favors indicates that he was no musician; only the shorter ballade and the rondeau had forms commonly set to music. The long stanzas were never used by Machaut, even for his ballades not set to music; at the same time, writers who were not musicians, like Froissart, Granson, and Deschamps, employed them regularly. The relative metrical uniformity and regularity of all of 'Ch's' poems suggest that they were composed near the same time, and that he was not at the time greatly inclined to metrical experiment. He was perhaps following the model of an older court poet such as Jean de le Mote, who in the same years wrote at least two ballades in the ten-line stanzas of 'Ch's' lyrics, one of which appears in the Pennsylvania manuscript. At the same time, it is clear that 'Ch' found the long stanza congenial; his poems profit from the opportunity to expatiate which it provides.

While we may assume that young 'Ch' read his poems at court, they would not have been taken as personal statements. With form and content highly conventional, the customary manner of presenting the lyrics must have been quite stylized; gesture and expressive intonation, when employed, were most likely exaggerated and histrionic. Obviously, the stylization would have in large part effaced both the age and gender of the poet-speaker; as performer he would have been free to assume any convenient age, sex, or stance. Accordingly, in his fifteen poems 'Ch' takes on the various personas of aspiring, hopeless, successful, and bereft lover, rejected lady, three daughters of Phoebus, spokesman for lovers, sympathetic friend of a dead and of a dying lover, and wise commentator on love.

The speaker's character once fixed, 'Ch' had less latitude in the statement his poems made; the general outlines are largely predictable. In the ballades this statement is often epitomized in the refrains which conclude each stanza. Some of the 'Ch' refrains are quite vivid and dramatic, as with the despairing lady's cry (V), 'Young, you loved me, and old, you had cast me off,' or the moan of the lover in his purgatory of desire (II), 'I melt and burn like wax does in the fire.' Other refrains function as simple recapitulations, as with the prayer of the friend who attends the lover's bier (XII), 'May God have mercy on his soul'; and the warm invocation of the successful lover (XIV), 'Grace to my lady and praise to Love.'

The refrain naturally divides the ballade into a three-part rhetorical structure, and 'Ch' made effective use of the division. The lover who melts like wax spends the first stanza describing his suffering, the second describing the source of the suffering, and the third asserting the lady's obduracy in the face of his loyal service. He thus focusses in easy progression on himself, then on the lady, and finally on their relationship to each other. In a similar neat progression the rejected lady begins by talking about her present state, 'alone, lost, deprived of all benefits' (l. 6); in the second stanza she recalls her once-happy life of love; and in the third she reproaches Venus for having led her into a secret love and to her ruin. The poem thus moves from the lady's present situation, to her past happiness, and at length to a slightly-veiled moral commentary about the fact that Venus—that is, sexual love—offers no protection against the lover's faithlessness. 'Ch's' other ballades have comparable structure which is readily analyzed; he handles the form with ease and grace.

The form of the chant royal offers more problems to the poet than the ballade does. Five long stanzas plus envoy, with a demanding rhyme scheme, but without refrain to define the stanza units, make lyric effectiveness difficult. The difficulty perhaps explains why the chant and related five-stanza types did not rival the ballade's popularity in Middle French even though they were the lineal descendants of the chanson, the dominant Old French lyric form. In 'Ch's' four chants royaux the stanzas tend to be parallel rather than juxtaposed or set in an order of progression as in his ballades. One of the chants (IV), for example, is simply a long prayer for lovers with each stanza containing one or more petitions. In stanza one the poet asks that various classes have their appropriate rewards: joy to ladies, pleasure to lovers, pain and torment to the envious. In two, developed by personification, he begs that ladies behave gently with their lovers:

> May Danger not have absolute lordship
> Nor Denial harsh strength;
> May Delay depart confronted with Good Will. (ll. 10–12)

In the ensuing stanzas he requests that ladies of beauty and modesty be rewarded with increased merit and virtue; calls on the natural order, the planets and elements, to favor the followers of Bonne Amour; and addresses his personal prayer to his lady, wishing her health and asked her pity. The envoy is but a line, 'My good comes from you, gracious born.'

In all four of 'Ch's' chants royaux the final stanza is a direct address by the speaker to his lady. This conforms to one feature of Froissart's practice, which in turn is built on the formulas of the *puys* of Picardy.[5] The effect of thus making the fifth stanza direct address is to extend the invocative and hortatory envoy back into the poem. Such extension works out relatively well in the chant I have just described, which is a prayer and accordingly hortatory *in toto*. But in the others it cuts short the arguments. For instance, in the chant devoted to the description of the sovereign life of love (I), after four stanzas extolling various features of this paradisal life, the shift to direct address in the fifth—though the poet handles the shift gracefully enough—has the effect of truncating thematic development.

All fifteen of 'Ch's' works, nevertheless, are effectively unified. The prominent practitioners of the Middle French lyric mode taught him to make his images clear and consistent, and not to fragment his poetic picture by mixing different kinds of images. Five of his poems (I–IV, IX) are built around little personification allegories; one of the chants (IX), for instance, features a parliament summoned by Love, in which Desire refutes Danger, and Pity puts Refusal to great confusion. Another six poems (V–VIII, X, XI) are built around literary reference. In the ballade of the bereft lover (VIII), he begins by comparing his lady to eleven famous ladies: Esther, Thisbe, Guinevere, etc.; in the second stanza, he compares himself to two ladies full of anguish, Phyllis and Io; and in the last he reviles 'horrible and insolent' Atropos, who has taken his beloved from him. The other four poems (XII–XV) are developed around single conventional images. One ballade of this type (XV) begins,

> Whoever would cut my heart in two
> Would see there the imprint of the lovely eyes
> Of my mistress.

After the speaker describes how Love has imprinted the portrait of the lady in his heart, he proceeds to elaborate on the beauty of her image, and then in the final stanza to offer thanksgiving to his eyes, Love, and the lady.

As I have said, 'Ch's' poems do not evidence any startling parallels with those of his putative associate Geoffrey Chaucer, but of course the conventions of the mode make interesting similarities inevitable. I might mention a few. 'Ch's' chant eulogizing the life of Bonne Amour (I) is quite like the song of Antigone in Book II of *Troilus* (ll. 827–75); the ballade petition for lovers (IV) is similar to the prayer of the narrator of *Troilus* near the beginning of Book I (ll. 21–49); the lament of the rejected lady (V) is very much in the spirit of Anelida's lament in *Anelida and Arcite*, as well as the complaints of several other of Chaucer's ladies; the bereft lover's enumeration of thirteen famous ladies (VIII) includes eight named in the ballade of the Prologue to the *Legend* (F.249–69); the parliament of Love in the chant royal (IX), which includes a special public plea by the lover, in some respects is like the gathering of personifications around the bier of Pity and the lover's ensuing bill of complaint in the *Complaint of Pity*; the testament of the languishing lover (XIII) is like that of Troilus in Book V (ll. 295–315); the narrator's call for sympathy in the same ballade is like a similar invocation in the *Complaint of Mars* (ll. 272–298); and the description of the lady whose image is imprinted in the lover's heart is comparable to the description of Blanche in the *Book of the Duchess* (ll. 848–1014), notably in its mingling of physical and moral attributes.

These parallels show mainly that 'Ch' and young Geoffrey Chaucer shared the same poetic mode. More indicative of 'Ch's' ability to move in the same

2. *University of Pennsylvania MS French 15, f.75v, showing rubrics of a ballade and a chant royal, with 'Ch' inserted (edited as Ch III and IV).*

literary circles with Geoffrey is the evidence of his lyrics in manifesting such Chaucerian qualities as grace, wit, liveliness, and integrity of poetic statement. The poems do possess these qualities to at least some degree, though they are perhaps partially concealed by the high degree of conventionality of the mode. So long as one recognizes that fine distinctions in use of personifications, a heavy burden of literary allusion, and dependence on commonplace images were given of this mode, he is in a good position to evaluate 'Ch's' success in utilizing such devices and tropes in his lyrics.

Two poems that make particularly judicious use of classical reference are perhaps more readily accessible to today's audience than the others. The eight-line rondeau presents a miniature *Ars Amatoria* by means of deft allusion. If you want to sacrifice to Venus in her proper temple, says the poem, you need to carry the arms to Orpheus, and to use Bacchus, Flora, and many promises—a transparent formula, gracefully presented, for capturing the lady with music, wine, flowers, and fast talk. The second poem is a ballade (VII) in which the lover-narrator, separated from his beloved by parents or perhaps husband, finds that he needs a desperate strategem to get together with her. In the poem the beloved is seen as a new Danäe imprisoned in a tower by suspicious Acrisius; the guard is Argus of a hundred eyes, who stood guard over Io for Juno; and the narrator sees no solution but for Jupiter to turn him into a shower of gold, just as the god metamorphosed himself to get to Danäe. In desiring to be changed into gold, the narrator is probably indicating that money offers the best means for him to realize his amorous ambitions, though he may simply be saying that he needs a miracle. In any event, the ballade represents another light and graceful use of classical images. Both of these poems are quite Ovidian, focussing much more on the practical aspects of love than the other thirteen do. Yet in the others too there is a fine poetic use of classical allusion to figurative effect, as in the lady's lament (V) in which the waters of Helicon, a place associated with the Muses, seem to be metaphorically equated with the lover's poetic activity. The fact that they stain the lady deeply thus has nice poetic force.

One touchstone for distinguishing a good fourteenth-century lyric poet from an ordinary one is found in the use of personifications. With good writers the abstractions are carefully discriminated and their allegorical interactions are thoroughly worked out. 'Ch' in fact is a thoughtful and inventive allegorist. In the ballade (III) in which the lover tells of receiving his lady's grace, for instance, the second stanza offers a fine representation of the psychological forces at work at his time of grace: The lady's Danger is in exile while her Pity is present in her prettiest dress; the lover's Fair Prayer employs Delight and Joy to forestall her Refusal; at the same time, his attention to Serve-Well puts to death her Delay and Shame (fear of censure); as a result, her debonnaire Heart returns from far away, and is moved to give him the name of Friend. In his chants especially (notably I, IV, and IX), 'Ch' introduces large casts of personifications, but not at random; each usually has a clear function in a coherent poetic picture.

Only one of the poems strikes me as patently mediocre, the chant royal (XI) which I entitle 'The Lady's Perfection.' It is probably mislabelled 'Ch', since it has notable differences from all the other works. Among the fourteen ballades and chants, it is the only one that does not have a rhyme scheme *ababb* for the first five lines of each stanza; it has the only envoy addressed to the 'prince of the puy';[6] and it is the only poem that makes use of anaphora throughout.[7] The effect of the last feature is excessiveness and banality. The contents otherwise are simple and uninteresting, and the presentation is uninventive. Some other poems have vexed passages which detract from them, particularly 'The Sovereign Life of Love' (I), in which the meaning is confused and uncertain in several places.[8] But the trouble with meaning here, as in other problematic passages of the works, probably has more to do with the scribe than with the poet.[9] Like the other 'Ch' works, 'The Sovereign Life' has a degree of complexity and interestingness that 'The Lady's Perfection' lacks. If 'Ch' is not Chaucer, he is yet a poet of talent who almost always handles well the traditional mode in which he is working.

Aside from the one chant, the consistency in quality of versification, image, and imaginative vision of the 'Ch' works supports the hypothesis that they were written by a single poet, probably near the same time. The metrics provide a more obvious feature that makes them appear to be a coherent set. As I have indicated, the rhyme schemes are quite uniform. Moreover, few other poems in Penn have the ten-line stanza found in nine of the fifteen lyrics, nor do many others have the related nine, eleven, and twelve-line stanzas found in five more.

Further indications about 'Ch' and the time and place of composition of these poems emerge from studying the collection as a whole and the other poems that it contains. The more important information, along with additional texts from Penn, is presented in the sections of this study that follow the texts and translations. As with no comparable manuscript, a great deal about Penn has particular significance for Chaucer, and all aspects have general relevance for the literary situation in his society. Similarly, the poems of 'Ch' both show what Chaucer's French verse might have been like and well exemplify the whole French lyric mode that prevailed in his time. Though they possess a certain individuality, in most ways they provide an epitome of the manuscript's literary contents.

TEXTS

[Ch I; MS #235]

Ch

    Entre les biens que creature humainne
    Puist acquerir pour vivre liement,
    C'est d'ensuir la vie souverainne
    D'Amours, qui est le droit commencement
5 De toute honneur; et amoureusement
    Eslire dame honnorable a maistresse;
    Et endurer, soit pour joie ou tristresse,
    Son bon plaisir et gracieux vouloir;
    Et par ainsi demenant ceste vie
10 Se puet en grace amoureuse veoir
    Dont tous biens vient et plaisance cherie.

2

    Car il est vray qu'en l'excellente demaine
    D'Amours regne gracieux Pensement,
    Franchise, Honnour, Esperance hautainne,
15 Foy, Loyauté, Leesse, Esbatement;
    Secours conforte Dangier prestement
    Quant Escondit le requerant trop blesce;
    Refus y maint par raisonnable adresce,
    Et Loing Detry, pour les bons percevoir
20 Ou Pitié vaint quant Bonne Amour l'otrie;
    Et la est Joie en signe de Vouloir,
    Vie aduree et de Joye enrichie.

3

    Et au seurplus, dame de graces plaine—
    Teles dont cuer d'amant joieusement
25 Se puet vivre—donne garison saine
    Par Doulz Regart et signes doulcement.
    La sont souspir getez couvertement,   [f.74d]
    La sont penser a l'espoir de leesce,
    La est aussi Souvenir qui ne cesse
30 Avec le vueil de servir main et soir,
    Et d'aviser comment dame et amie
    A de garir vray amant le pouoir
    A cemonse de Doulce Courtoisie.

TRANSLATION

The Sovereign Life of Love

One of the good things that a human being
May do in order to live happily
Is to follow the sovereign life
Of Love, which is the true beginning
Of all honor; and in accordance with Love
To choose an honorable lady as his mistress;
And to endure, whether for joy or sadness,
Her good pleasure and gracious will;
By thus leading this life,
Through the grace of Love he will be able to perceive
The source of all good things and of dear pleasure.

For it is true that in the excellent domain
Of Love gracious Thought reigns,
Generosity, Honor, high Hope,
Faith, Loyalty, Joy, Diversion;
Help soothes Danger quickly
When Denial wounds the petitioner too much;
Refusal and Long Delay remain there according to propriety,
So that he may appreciate the benefits
When Good Love allows Pity to conquer;
There is Joy the mark of Desire,
There is a stable life enriched with Joy.

And what is more, the lady full of graces—
Those graces that make the heart of a lover
Able to live joyously—grants complete health sweetly
By Sweet Looks and signs.
There are sighs breathed covertly,
There are thoughts hoping for happiness,
There also is unceasing Memory
Together with the wish to serve morning and evening,
And to meditate how his lady and friend
Has the power to heal a true lover
At the instance of Sweet Courtesy.

4

Pour ce conclus en voulenté certainne
35 D'Amours servir et ma dame humblement,
Qu'il n'est vie de vices si lointainne,
N'estat si gay que d'amer loyaument.
Car par amer puet on habondanment
Acquerir joie en haultainne noblesce,
40 Par Bien Amer s'eslongn'on de l'apresce
A deshonnour. Assez est assavoir
De Bien Amer entrer en seignourie:
De miex dire, de miex faire et valoir.
S'est eureux qui a ce point s'allie.

5

45 Toute belle, de grace droite plaine,
Gente a devis, au maintien excellent,
Dame que j'aim, melodie mondainne!
A voir l'estat de vo gentilz corps gent,
A vous servir—gracieuse en simplesce,
50 Riche d'atour, avisee en jeunesse—
Si liegement qu'en ce point vueil manoir.
N'autre de vous n'y clamerai partie
Car Loyauté en fera tel devoir
Qu'assez sera pour mener vie lie.

L'envoy

55 S'Amours me veult de ses hauls biens pourvoir
De Joie aray joieuse compaignie.

16 conforte] confort a
42 entrer] en tron
48 or 49 line missing
52 clamerai] clamera

[Ch II; MS #237]

Balade [f.75a]

Ch

Onques doulour ne fu plus angoisseuse
Que mon las cuer endure nuit et jour,
Ne tristesce plus aspre ne crueuse.
Morir m'est joie et brief finer doulçour,
5 Confort d'ami m'est de nulle valour,

For this reason I resolve with sure will
To serve Amour and my lady humbly,
For there is no life so far from vice,
Nor state so gay as that of loving loyally.
For by loving one may gain abundant
Joy in high nobility.
By Good Loving one draws himself away from the bitterness
Of dishonour. To enter into the lordship
Of Good Loving, this is enough to know:
To speak better, to do better, to increase in merit.
He is happy who joins this life.

Completely lovely one, full of true grace,
Pretty as one could choose, of excellent bearing,
Lady that I love, earthly melody!
To observe your noble person,
To serve you—gracious and unaffected,
Rich of attire, discreet in youth—
So dutifully that I may remain in that position;
No other thing will I ask of you,
For Loyalty will do such duty
That this will suffice me to lead a happy life.

If Love wishes to provide me with his high benefits,
I will have the joyous company of Joy.

The Lover Who Melts Like Wax

Never was there more wretched sorrow
Than what my poor heart endures night and day,
Nor sadness more bitter and cruel;
To die is joy to me and a quick end sweetness;
Ami's comfort is of no value to me;

Espoir n'a cause aux drois de ma leesce,
Car le vouloir de ma belle maistresse
Est de mon cuer faire vivre en martire.
Quanque j'en ay me martrist, tue, et blesce,
10 Que fons et fris comme au feu fait la cire.

2

Ses rians yeulx, sa maniere joieuse,   [f.75b]
Son doulx regart, son gracieux atour,
Sa grant beauté, sa parole amoureuse,
Son plaisant corps, et sa fresche coulour
15 Ne me donnent en tous lieux que doulour,
Ne par eux n'ay de reconfort adresce.
Com plus la voy, plus li di ma maistresse.
N'ains y perçoy sa grace, Dieu li mire.
Refus y croist et Pitié pour moy cesse
20 Que fons et fris, etc.

3

Et assez puet sa doulceur gracieuse
Congnoistre que loyaument, sans fauls tour,
L'aim, criens, et sers pour sa treseüreuse
Mercy avoir, en gardant son honnour.
25 Mais com je croy Dangier la fait sejour
Avec Reffus, par quoy elle me lesse
Plain de souspirs et de plains, en la presse
De Desiriers, ou Desespoir se tire
Si qu'emmy moy tout desconfort s'adresce,
30 Que fons, etc.

[Ch III; MS #239]

                        Balade   [f.75c]

Ch

Je cuide et croy qu'en tous les joieux jours
Que le soleil cler et net sueil parer,
Et les heures faire leur commun cours
Pour nuit obscure a son droit amener,
5 Celui fu bon—je le doy honorer!
Gay, gent, plaisant, et de grace adjourna;
Phebus aussi de doulçour l'aourna,

14

Hope has no power to further my happiness,
For the desire of my beautiful mistress
Is to make my heart live in martyrdom.
Whatever I have from her martyrs, kills, and wounds me,
And I melt and burn like wax does in the fire.

Her laughing eyes, her happy manner,
Her sweet look, her gracious attire,
Her great beauty, her words of love.
Her pleasant body, and her fresh complexion
Give me in all places only sorrow,
Nor by them have I a way to comfort.
The more I see her, the more I call her my mistress.
I have never found grace in her, God protect her.
Refusal grows in her and Pity for me stops
So that I melt and burn like wax does in the fire.

And well might her gracious sweetness
Recognize that I love, fear, and serve her
Loyally, without deceit, in order to gain
Her most joyful Mercy, while guarding her honor.
However, I believe that Danger stays with her
With Refusal; by them she leaves me
Full of sighs and moans, in the oppression
Of Desire, where Despair advances,
So that within me all discomfort grows,
And I melt and burn like wax does in the fire.

The Day of Grace

I think and believe that among all the joyful days
That the clear, bright sun is wont to adorn,
When the hours make their common course
And lead dark night to its own land,
That day was good—I must honor it!
It dawned gay, noble, pleasant, and gracious;
Phebus also adorned it with sweetness,

15

Et le moment de ses biens enrichi
Chascun des diex, son pouoir li donna,
10 Quant ma dame me donna nom d'Ami.

2

Pitié se mist en ses plus biaux atours,
Et en excil fu Dangier oultre mer.
Confort, Deduit, Leesce, Gay Secours
Firent Refus par Bel Prier finer.
15 Cuer debonnaire et digne d'onnorer
Vint de moult loins ou pays par de ça—
Loyal Penser de droit l'i envoia;
Et Bien Servir mist a mort Long Detry
Et Honte, avec qui fuï ça et la,
20 Quant ma dame, etc.

3

Dont j'en loe sur toute rien Amours,
Et la doulçour de ma dame sans per,
A qui je doy de droit toutes honnours,
Servir, cremir, et loyaument amer—   [f.75d]
25 Son vueil li viengne a son bon desirer—
Si vraiement qu'autre n'ameray ja.
L'eure fu bonne et Amours l'ordena,
Et pour moy fu renouvelé Mercy
Qui humblement s'aparu et monstra
30 Quant ma dame, etc.

[Ch IV; MS #240]

Chançon Royal   [f.75d]

Ch

Aux dames joie, et aux amans plaisance,
Et a Amours reverence et honnour;
Aux envieux toute paine et grevance,
Et au surplus aux mesdisans langour
5 Tous temps aviengne; et secours de Doulçour
Soit ottroiés de puissance amoureuse
Aux vrais servans sans chose dolereuse.
Pitié leur soit advocate aprestee
Et par servir Mercy guerredonnee.

16

And each of the gods endowed the moment
With his benefits, and gave it his power,
When my lady gave me the name of Friend.

Pity came forth in her prettiest attire,
While Danger was in exile overseas;
Comfort, Delight, Joy, and Happy Help,
With Fair Prayer made Refusal stop;
The debonnaire Heart, worthy of honor,
Came from far away to this country—
Loyal Thought sent her here, as was right;
And Serve-Well put to death both Long Delay
And Shame, with whom I had fled hither and yon,
When my lady gave me the name of Friend.

Therefore I praise Love above all for it,
And the sweetness of my peerless lady,
To whom by right I owe all honor,
To serve, fear, and love loyally—
May her desire be fulfilled according to her good wish—
So truly that I will never love another.
The hour was good, Love ordained it;
For me Mercy was renewed
Who modestly appeared and revealed herself
When my lady gave me the name of Friend.

A Prayer for Lovers

Joy to ladies, and pleasure to lovers,
And reverence and honor to Love;
All pain and torment to the envious,
And what is more may feebleness
Ever afflict slanderers; and may the aid of Sweetness
Be granted by Love's power
To true servants, with nothing sad.
May Pity be their prompt advocate
And Mercy their reward for service.

10 Dangier n'y ait seignourie a oultrance,
Ne Escondit rigoreuse vigour;
Detry se parte au fait de Bienveillance,
Entendue de Bon Cuer la clamour.
Honte n'y soit message ne Dolour;
15 Reffus n'y puist oster Vie Joieuse;
Paour seüre ait cause gracieuse
De congnoistre Loiauté esprouvee
Ou temps qu'estre doit grace recouvree.

3

A plaisant corps, a gaie contenance,
20 A vis paré d'une fresche coulour,
A biau maintien, a joieuse samblance,
A cuer loial, a port de gent atour,
A simplesce d'excellente valour,
A maniere de meffait paoureuse,
25 Et a dame digne d'estre eüreuse
Par bien faire, par bien estre aournee,   [f.76a]
Croisse valour de vertu redoublee.

4

Sugetté soit naturelle ordonnance
Aux parties ensivans Bonne Amour:
30 Fueille, flour, fruit de leesce, habondance,
Et quanqu'il est de tout bon a ce jour;
Les elemens n'y soient a sejour
Pour eulx servir, et n'y soit dangereuse
Planete, en rier, dure, ne despiteuse,
35 Pour vouloir ce qu'il leur plaist et agree
En fait, en dit, en cuer, et en pensee.

5

Et a vous, dame, ou toute m'esperance
Maint, et qu'en bien je cheris et honnour,
Soit encliné Bonne Perseverance,
40 Grace, Santé; et si face retour
Loial Voloir pour manoir en millour
Estat de joie. Et vers moy si piteuse
Soies que loins soit de dolours crueuse
Le cuer de moy, belle tresdesiree,
45 Que j'ameray tant que j'aray duree.

L'envoy

Mon bien de vous vient, gracieuse nee.

32 sejour] ce jour

18

May Danger not have absolute lordship
Nor denial harsh strength;
May Delay depart at the instance of Good Will,
The plaint of the Good Heart having been heard.
May neither Shame nor Sorrow be messenger;
May Refusal not dislodge the joyful life;
May Fear reassured have a pleasing reason
To recognize proven Loyalty
At the time when grace should be obtained.

To the pleasant body, to the gay countenance,
To the face adorned with fresh complexion,
To fine conduct, to joyous appearance,
To the loyal heart, to noble manner,
To modesty of excellent worth,
To conduct fearful of misdeed,
And to the lady worthy of happiness
For doing well, for fine adornment,
May merit increase redoubled by virtue.

May the natural order be subject
To those who follow Good Love:
Leaf, flower, fruit of joy, abundance,
And whatever there is of every good this day;
May the elements not hold back
From serving them, and the planet not be reluctant,
Retrograde, cruel, nor dispiteous
In desiring what will please and suit them
In deed, in word, in heart, and in thought.

And to you, lady, in whom all my hope
Remains, and whom I cherish and honor dearly,
May Good Perseverance be propitious,
And Grace, and Health; and also may Loyal Desire
Return so you may live in the highest state of joy.
And may you be so piteous toward me
That my heart will be far from cruel sorrows,
Beautiful, most desirable one,
Whom I will love so long as I live.

My good comes from you, born gracious.

Balade [f.76a]

Ch

Fauls Apyus, pires que Lichaon,
Sans foy, sans droit, compaignon de Judas,
Cuers d'Erode, voulenté de Noiron,
Je vail Dido parlant a Eneas,
5 Lasse et deserte; ainsi laissié m'as
Seule, esgaree, ou de tous biens mendie
A cuer dolent et a couleur changie,
Plus que triste, de maulx avironnee. [f.76b]
Ma plaisance est voie desesperee.
10 En povreté gist la fin de ma vie,
Car cuer de pierre a perverse pensee.
Jone, m'amas, et vieille, m'as guerpie.

2

Usee suis et en chetivoisin,
Servant de ce dont jadis me gardas.
15 De moy veoir, abhominacion!
Par tez samblans te moustre plus que las.
Ou sont les chans que ja pieça chantas?
Ou est le temps que la flour fu queillie
Soubz le ruissel de la fontaine Helie?
20 De la liquer trop m'a descoulouree
Ou par tez dis j'estoie asseüree,
Desquelz je suis appertement trahie,
Car sans raison, de tristresse affublee,
Jone, etc.

3

25 Ma simplesce donna audicion
A ton faint cuer et tant que tu trouvas
Medee vraye. Or ay trouvé Jasson
En faussesté que ja ne laisseras.
Venus, Venus, trop est las le solas,
30 Car tes brandons ont ma coulour noircie.
Pourquoy ne fu l'aventure anoncie
Du bel Helaine et celui de Medee,
Quant tu me fis jadis l'amour celee
Qui a present me tolt plaisance lie?
35 Di moy pourquoy ou je suis esgaree.
Jone, m'amas, et vieille, m'as guerpie.

1 The story of the false judge Apius is found in Livy's *History*, III; *Roman de la Rose*, ed. Lecoy, ll. 5559–5628; and Chaucer's Physician's Tale. Ovid tells the story of the impious Lycaon, *Metamorphoses*, I, 198–243.

3 d'Erode] de Rode   31 ne fu] me fu
18–19 reversed in MS   33 fis] fus

20

The Castoff Lady

False Apius, worse than Lichaon,
Without faith, without justice, fellow of Judas,
Heart of Herod, will of Nero,
I am like Dido speaking to Aeneas,
Dejected and deserted. Thus have you left me
Alone, lost, where I am deprived of all good,
With sorrowing heart and changed complexion,
More than sad, beset by evils;
My pleasure is a path of despair;
In poverty lies the end of my life,
For a heart of stone has wicked thought;
Young, you loved me, and old, you have cast me off.

I am spent and in misery,
Servant of that from which you formerly protected me.
To see me, abomination!
By your looks you prove yourself worse than a wretch.
Where are the songs that you used to sing?
Where is the time that the flower was gathered
Beside the stream of the fountain of Helicon?
It stained me deeply with its waters
When by your song I was made confident.
By these I am openly betrayed,
Deprived of justice, shrouded with sadness.
Young, you loved me, and old, you have cast me off.

My innocence gave ear
To your deceitful heart until you found
A true Medea. Now I have found a Jason
In the falsity which you will never abandon.
Venus, Venus, your pleasure is too wretched,
For your torch has blackened my complexion.
Why was I not told the tale
Of the beautiful Helen and that of Medea
When earlier you incited me to the secret love
Which now takes joyful delight from me?
Tell me why I am thrown aside.
Young, you loved me, and old, you have cast me off.

balade [f.76b]

Ch

Nous, qui sommes trois filles a Phebus,
Et que Clemene a un jour enfanta,
Alectiez du pur lait Zephirus
O biau vergier que Damïen planta,
5   Devons loer celui qui nous crea,   [f.76c]
Le jour aussi de no prime naissance,
Car nous avons de droit tant de puissance
Que nostre espoux en qui maint seignourie.
Nous avec li vainquera sans doubtance
10 Viel Saturnus et sa dure lignie.

2

De nostre acort avons Palanurus,
Et Jupiter qui jadis li osta,
Ce dont en mer fu creée Venus.
Mars son biau chief pour no bien armera;
15 Le char gemmé ja Pheton n'amenra.
Thaïs converse onnera sa samblance;
Toutes ninphes voldront no bien veillance.
Crete, Colcos, Parguste, et Archadie
Feront finer et tiront a outrance
20 Viel Saturnus, etc.

3

Les diex de mer, et en chief Neptunus,
Et ceulx des bois, ou moult deduis [y] a,
Atremperont les eles d'Eolus,
Et Jupiter ses fouldres fondera.
25 Ainsi de nous chascune se verra
Menee a fin de mainte desplaisance.
Vive celui ou maint nostre esperance
Et qui pere de nous sa monarchie,
Le quel tira en bas par sa vaillance
30 Viel Saturnus et sa dure lignie.

1–2 The daughters of Apollo and Clymene are the Heliades, sisters of Phaeton: but they are five in number. There may be a confusion here with the three Graces, who were the daughters of Jupiter and Eurynome; Eurynome's daughter Leucothoe was also loved by Phoebus. The character of the Graces, attendants of Venus, might help the sense of the poem, but the uncertainty of the husband's identify (l. 8) leaves the final meaning a puzzle.
4 In Greek mythology Damia is equated with Demeter, the Roman Ceres, goddess of the fields.
11 Palanurus] Palamirus   24 fondera] forgera
13 creée] cree   28 qui] que

22

A New Golden Age

We who are three daughters of Phoebus,
Whom Clymene gave birth to in one day,
Nursed with the pure milk of Zephirus
In the beautiful garden that Damia planted—
We must praise him who created us,
Also the day of our first birth,
For we have by right as much power
As our spouse in whom lordship resides.
Undoubtedly with him we will conquer
Old Saturn and his cruel progeny.

In our party are Palinurus,
And Jupiter who of old carried him away,
He who created Venus in the sea.
Mars will arm his handsome head in our cause;
No longer will Phaeton guide the jewelled chariot;
Thaïs converted will honor her beauty;
All nymphs will wish us kindness;
Crete, Colchis, Parguste, and Arcadia
Will bring to an end and decisively overthrow
Old Saturn and his cruel progeny.

The gods of the sea, with Neptune in the lead,
And those of the woods, where there is much delight,
Will quiet the wings of Eolus,
And Jupiter will break his thunderbolt.
Thus each of us will find herself
Brought to the last of many displeasures.
May he thrive in whom our hope rests,
And who graces his kingdom with us.
Through his power he will throw down
Old Saturn and his cruel progeny.

Balade [f.77c]

Ch

Plus a destroit, et en plus forte tour
Qu'Acrisiüs n'enclost Dane jadis,
Est enclose la belle que j'aour
Comme mon dieu ou mondain paradis.
5   Car Argus est sus haulte roche assis
Ou nul des yeulx ne clot, et s'en a cent.
Se ne puis veir ma dame vraiement,
Ne ne verray, ce sçay je sans doubter,
Se Jupiter, a cui mon cuer s'atent,
10 Ne me fait brief en pluie d'or muer;

2

Et ce seroit certes le meilleur tour
Considerer, que la garde a tousdiz
Cuer Tantalus, et ara chascun jour,
Car de ce cas l'a Juno tout espris.
15 Or est il vray qu'a la tresbelle pris
Me sui rendu comme sien liegement,
Mais je sçay bien que jamais nullement
N'en aray rien qui me puist conforter
Se Jupiter, a cui mon cuer s'atent,
20 Ne me fait, etc.,

3

Comme il fist soy pour acquerir l'amour
De la gente Dane au tresriant vis,
Par qui Juno fu longtemps en doulour,
Et pour Yo et mainte autre a devis.
25 Si qu'en ce point je languiray, mendis
Des drois d'Amours, en angoisseux tourment.
Mes biens seront divers gemissement,
Et mes joies tourneront en amer,
Se Jupiter, a cui mon cuer s'atent,
30 Ne me fait brief en pluie d'or muer.

24

A Petition to Jupiter

Shut in a narrower cell and in a stronger tower
Than Acrisius shut Danäe in of old
Is the beautiful lady that I adore
As my god of the earthly paradise.
Argus is seated on a high rock
Where he closes none of his eyes, and he has a hundred.
Truly I cannot see my lady,
Nor will I see her, I know this without doubt,
Unless Jupiter, to whom my heart inclines,
Soon turns me into a shower of gold;

And this surely would be the best plan
To devise, since the guard has ever,
And ever will have, the heart of Tantalus,
Because in this affair Juno has fully roused him.
Now it is sure that I have given myself
To the most beautiful one as her liege,
But I know well that never in any way
Will I have anything that can comfort me
Unless Jupiter, to whom my heart inclines,
Soon turns me into a shower of gold,

As he did himself to acquire the love
Of the noble Danäe of the smiling face,
Because of whom Juno was long in sorrow,
As well as for Io and a great many others.
Thus in this state I will languish, deprived
Of the rights of Love, in anguished torment;
My pleasures will be varied sighs,
And my joys will turn to bitterness,
Unless Jupiter, to whom my heart inclines,
Soon turns me into a shower of gold.

Ch

Humble Hester, courtoise, gracieuse,
Belle Judith, plaisant a regarder,
Simple Tisbé, lie, gente, amoureuse,
Noble Helaine, Polixné en parler,
5   Lealle Hero, des autres la nomper,
Vraye Adriane, Yseut par biaux atours,
Noble Dido, Genievre en nobles mours,
Dane en valour, par tousdiz fuïr blasme—
Et celle dont venoient mes bons jours
10   Pourrist en terre, et je remains sans dame.

2

A cuer marry, a vie doulereuse,
Larmes aux yeulx, loins de joie esperer,
Au flun Cyron ou Philis angoisseuse
M'est exemplaire a mon las deviser,
15   Yo brute veult a moy deviser,
Triste, cornue, attainte de doulours.
Mais c'est pour ce: considerer tous jours
Que la belle qui cuer et corps m'entame,
Ma maistresse plainne d'umbles honnours,
20   Pourrist en terre, etc.

3

Mal m'as servi, orrible et despiteuse
Atropos, preste a me devourer.
Gouffre sans droit, murdriere fameilleuse,
Fisses l'Essient Nature dominer,
25   En jeune estate Leesse habondonner,
Par demener amoureuses doulçours.
Car jamais jour ne quier avoir secours,
Joie d'Amours, ne rien qui m'en enflame,
Puis que celle que j'amay par amours
30   Pourrist, etc.

17 jours] tours
24 Fisses] Eusses

The Bereft Lover

Modest Esther, courteous, gracious,
Beautiful Judith, pleasant to contemplate,
Simple Thisbe, happy, lovely, amorous,
Noble Helen, Polyxena in speaking,
Loyal Hero, nonpareil of all,
Faithful Ariadne, Isolt in fine apparel,
Noble Dido, Guinevere in noble customs,
Daphne in worth, ever shunning blame—
This one from whom came my good days
Decays in the ground, and I am left without my lady.

With unhappy heart, with sorrowful life,
Tears in my eyes, far from hope of joy,
I am at the river of Charon where Phyllis full of anguish
Provides an example for my desperate plan.
Io became brute is a model for me,
Unhappy, horned, stricken by sorrows.
Always it will be thus: to ponder every day
That the beautiful one who pierces my body and heart,
My mistress full of modest honor,
Decays in the ground, and I am left without my lady.

You have served me evilly, horrible and insolent
Atropos, ready to devour me,
Abyss without justice, famished murderer.
You have caused Knowledge to overcome Nature,
Youth to abandon Gaiety,
The enjoyment of amorous sweetnesses.
For never a day will I seek to have a remedy,
Joy of Love, or anything which will enflame me with it,
Since she whom I loved truly
Decays in the ground, and I am left without my lady.

Chanson Royal [f.78c]

Ch

    Pour les hauls biens amoureux anoncier,
    Et les vrais cuers des amans resjoïr,
    Et les graces qui y son publirer—
    Lesquelles ont par loiaulment servir—
5   Tout serviteur apresté d'obeïr
    Est apparu par mandement de Joye;
    Q'umble Pitié, qui de secours est voie,
    A plain pouoir et dominacion
    De donner ce qui les leaux conjoie:
10 Et c'est mercy sans contradiction.

2

    Et l'acort joieusement traïctier
    Fu Franchise cemonse de Desir,
    Qui debati a toutes fins Dangier
    Tant qu'il ne pot sa requeste obtenir.
15 Ou parlement qu'Amours fist par plaisir
    Fu Doulx Penser, qui doulcement s'emploie;
    Et Souvenir, que ne flenchist ne ploie,
    Avec Espoir la ot audicion.
    Pour les amans Pitié la si s'emploie
20 Qui a Reffus fist grant confusion

3

    En remonstrant le mal partout entier
    Que Detry fay a maint amant souffrir,
    Et que plains, plours, et souspir darrenier
    Viennent souvent desserte remerir;
25 Si qu'il couvient a ce cas prouveïr,
    Comme dit est, car Amours si anoie,   [f.78d]
    Et messagiere en aucuns lieux mennoie
    Ou Beauté regne et Doulce Impression.
    A cui je parle, et fay tant et maistroie
30 Que de Dangier je banis l'opinion.

4

    'Dont, reguarde que volu tramblier!
    Atant, Pitié, vueillons nous tous offrir
    Au service d'Amours; et acointier
    Leal Vouloir, Amoureux Souvenir,

The Parliament of Love

In order to proclaim the exalted benefits of Love,
And to rejoice the true hearts of lovers,
And to announce the graces that are in it—
Those that lovers have through loyal service—
Every servant ready to obey
Appeared by the command of Joy;
And humble Pity, who is the way of succor,
Possessed full power and dominion
To bestow that which delights the loyal ones:
Without contradiction, that is mercy.

And for negotiating an agreement joyously
Generosity was summoned by Desire,
Who challenged Danger at all points
So that he could not have his way.
In this parliament that Love assembled to his pleasure
There was Sweet Thought, who sweetly occupied herself;
And Memory, who neither turned aside nor yielded,
Together with Hope there had a hearing.
Pity too busied herself there for lovers
And she put Refusal to great confusion

In protesting the complete evil
That Delay everywhere causes many a lover to suffer,
And the fact that complaints, tears, and sighs
Often come in the end to reward merit;
Thus it is necessary to provide for this case,
As is said, since Love is so troubling
And sends his embassy to every place
That Beauty and Sweet Impression reign.
To whom [Pity] I spoke, and so managed and gained mastery
That I overcame the influence of Danger:

'Now look upon us trembling!
At this time, Pity, we all want to offer ourselves
To the service of Love; and to make the acquaintance
Of Loyal Desire and Amorous Memory,

35 Cuer pacient pour le vue soustenir
De nos dames se Refus nous guerroie;
Et esperer, se Dangier les fourvoie,
Souffrir tousdis et servir de cuer bon
Feront fenir leur durté qui desvoie
40 Et en met maint en desolacion.'

5

Dame, a beauté digne de moult prisier,
S'il vous plaisoit a mes maulx secourir,
Mon bien seroit en estat d'essaucier,
Et mon vray cuer en l'espoir de jouir.
45 Mais s'il vous plaist le propos maintenir
Ou le vostre des longtemps a seurploie,
Riens ne sera certes qui me resjoie.
Si vous requier par grace guerredon;
S'aray le bien que pieça desiroie
50 Et de confort gaie provision.

L'envoy

Princes, Amours veult qu'on sache et qu'on voie
Qu'il n'est vie que d'amer, ce n'est mon.

17 flenchist] flechist
31 This line is a syllable short and does not make sense as it stands. The translation represents a guess as to the intended meaning.

[Ch X; MS #260]

Rondel [f.80d]

Ch

Qui veult faire sacrefice a Venus
Ou temple dont elle est droite deesse,
Porter couvient les armes Orpheus—
Qui veult faire sacrefice a Venus—
5 Et espandre des hautains biens Bacchus,
Et de Flora don, et mainte promesse—
Qui veult faire sacrefice a Venus [f.81a]
Ou temple dont elle est droite deesse.

30

Our hearts being patient to sustain the sight
Of our ladies if Refusal makes war on us,
And to hope, if Danger thrusts them aside,
That constant endurance and willing service
Will make their cruelty cease, which bewilders
And leads many to desolation.'

Lady of beauty, worthy of great esteem,
If it pleased you to help my troubles
My soul would be in a state of exaltation,
And my true heart in hope of enjoyment.
But if it pleases you to maintain the resolution
In which your heart has long remained,
There is indeed nothing that will gladden me.
So I ask guerdon of your grace,
And I will have the good that I long desired
And provision of happy comfort.

Prince, Love wishes it to be known and seen
That there is no life except that of love, indeed.

How to Sacrifice in Venus' Temple

He who wants to sacrifice to Venus
In the temple of which she is proper goddess,
Must carry the arms of Orpheus—
He who wants to sacrifice to Venus—
And he must pour forth the great gifts of Bacchus,
And the bounty of Flora, and many a promise—
He who wants to sacrifice to Venus
In the temple of which she is proper goddess.

Chançon Royal [f.81b]

Ch

 Venez veoir qu'a fait Pymalion;
 Venez veoir excellente figure;
 Venez veoir l'amie de Jason;
 Venez veoir bouche a poy d'ouverture;
5 Venez veoir de Hester la bonté;
 Venez veoir de Judith la Beauté;
 Venez veoir les doulz yeulz Dame Helaine;
 Venez oïr doulce voix de Serainne;
 Venez veoir Polyxene la Blonde;
10 Venez veoir de plaisance la plaine,
 Qui n'a de tout pareille ne seconde. [f.81c]

2

 Avisez bien sa gente impression;
 Avisez bien sa maniere seüre;
 Avisez bien l'imaginacion
15 De son gent corps a joieuse estature;
 Avisez bien sa lie humilité;
 Avisez bien sa simple gaieté;
 Avisez bien comment de biens est plaine;
 Avisez bien sa faiture hautaine;
20 Avisez bien comment elle suronde
 En meurs, en sens, au tant que dame humaine
 Qui soit vivant a ce jour en ce monde.

3

 Ymaginez humble condicion
 Qui la maintient en parfaite mesure
25 Si qu'en elle a de tout bel et tout bon,
 Au tant que dame ou vaillance prent cure.
 Ymaginez sa gracieuseté;
 Ymaginez son sens amoderé;
 Ymaginez l'excellence hautainne
30 De son estat que Leesce a bien mainne,
 Et vous direz, 'Vela dame ou habonde
 Honnour, savoir, avis, joie mondaine,
 Sens, simplesce, bonté, et beauté monde.'

32

The Lady's Perfection

Come see what Pygmalion has made;
Come see the excellent form;
Come see the loved one of Jason;
Come see the little mouth;
Come see the goodness of Esther;
Come see the beauty of Judith;
Come see the sweet eyes of Lady Helen;
Come hear the sweet voice of the Siren;
Come see Polyxena the Blonde;
Come see the fullness of pleasure,
Who has among all no equal nor second.

Study well her noble figure;
Study well her assured manner;
Study well the image
Of her noble body of joyful stature;
Study well her happy humility;
Study well her modest grace;
Study well how she is full of goodness;
Study well her high creation;
Study well how she excels
In character, in wisdom, as much as any lady
Who is living at this day in this world.

Imagine her modest bearing
Which maintains perfect moderation
So that in her is all beautiful and good,
As much as any lady in whom worth is of concern.
Imagine her graciousness;
Imagine her temperate good sense;
Imagine the high excellence
Of her position, which Joy guides toward good,
And you will say, 'Here is a lady in whom abounds
Honor, wisdom, judgement, worldly joy,
Understanding, modesty, goodness, and flawless beauty.'

C'est ma dame dont j'atens guerredon;
35 C'est mon confort; c'est ma pensee pure;
C'est mon espoir; c'est la provision
Des hautains biens en qui je m'asseüre;
C'est ma joie, mon secours, ma santé,
Mon riche vuet, de long temps desiré,
40 Mon doulx ressort, ma dame souveraine;
C'est celle aussi qui tous les jours m'estraine
De la joieuse et tresamoureuse onde
De qui Penser avient du droit demaine
De Loyauté, que Leesce areonde.

5

45 Dame que j'aim, flour de perfection,
Rousee en May, soleil qui tousdis dure,
Flun de doulçour, a cui comparoison
D'autre dame belle ne s'amesure
Quant a mon veuil ne a ma voulenté,
50 Si vrayement que mi bien sont enté
En vous du tout. Ne soit de vous lointainne
Pitié pour moy, donner garison sainne,
Car trop seroit ma tristresce parfonde
S'elle n'estoit de vostre cuer prochainne,
55 Fuiant Dangier que Bonne Amour confonde.

L'envoy [f.81d,bottom]

Princes du puy, savez vous qu'i demainne
Ma dame en bien a joieuse faconde,
Et ce qu'elle est? De Deduit chievetainne,
Si que la voir les cuers de vices monde.

40 Mon] A mon
43 avient] venant
59 que] qua

She is my lady from whom I await reward;
She is my comfort; she is my pure thought;
She is my hope; she is the provision
Of the exalted benefits in which I find security.
She is my joy, my help, my health,
My rich wish, long desired,
My sovereign lady, my sweet refuge;
She it is also who all the days keeps me
In the joyous and very amourous sea
In which Thought comes from the true domain
Of Loyalty, which Delight surrounds.

Lady that I love, flower of perfection,
Dew in May, sun which lasts ever,
Well of sweetness, to whom there is no measure
Of comparison with other beautiful ladies,
Either in my desire or my will,
So truly is my good rooted
Completely in you. May Pity for me not be
Far from you, to give me complete healing,
For my sadness would be too deep
If she were not close to your heart,
Fleeing Danger which confounds Good Love.

Prince of the puy, do you know what governs
My lady in goodness in joyous plenty,
And what she is? Sovereign of Delight,
So that seeing her cleanses hearts of vice.

[Ch XII; MS #273]

Balade

[f.84b]

Ch

    Mort le vy d'ire, et si n'i avoit ame
    Qui pour son bien se voulsist traveillier.
    Je vi son corps sans vie mis soubz lame,
    Ou escript ot, 'Ci gist l'amant entier
5   Qui onques jour ne pot, pour Bel Prier,
    A sa doulour trouver Joieux Secours.
    Cuer sans pitié li a finé ses jours;
    Onques si vray ne reposa en corps;
    Certes, il est leal martir d'Amours—
10 A son ame soit Dieu misericors.'

2

    Car il amoit loiaument sans nul blasme,
    Bel a son dit et bon a son cuidier,
    Mais je sçay que onques a nul jour fame
    Ne fist si mal par trop croire Dangier.
15 Il avoit sens et vouloir sans changier;
    Souvent baignoit son vis pale de plours;
    C'estoit pitié a oïr ses clamours;
    Jamais de tel ne sera fais restors.
    Or est il mort, assegiez de dolours—
20 A son ame soit Dieu misericors.

3

    De son vray cuer fist present a sa dame—
    Ce fu la fin de son jour derrenier—
    Disant ainsi, 'Puis que d'Amours la flame
    Me fait du tout a vie renoncier,
25 A Dieu commant celle que tant ay chier,
    A Dieu commant plaisancë et baudours.'
    Lors clost les yeulx en perdant ses coulours.
    Amours servi et en fin en est mors.
    [Last two lines missing in manuscript.]

1 si] se
12 Bel . . . bon] Belle . . . bonne
13 que onques] conques

36

Requiem for a Lover

I see him dead from anguish, and there was no soul
Who would exert itself for his good.
I see his lifeless body placed beneath the slab,
On which it is written, 'Here lies the complete lover
Who never was able, through Fair Request,
To find Happy Help for his sorrow.
A heart without pity ended his days;
Never so true a one lived in a body;
Truly he is a loyal martyr of Love—
May God have mercy on his soul.'

Indeed he loved loyally without any blame,
Lovely in his word, and good in his thought,
And I know that never at any time did a lady
Do so badly through trusting in Danger too much.
He had understanding and an unchanging will;
He often bathed his pale visage in tears;
It was a pity to hear his cries;
Never will he be healed of these.
Now he is dead, beset by sorrows—
May God have mercy on his soul.

He made a present of his true heart to his lady—
This was at the end of his last day—
Speaking thus, 'Since the flame of Love
Makes me abandon life for good,
I commend to God she whom I held so dear;
I commend to God pleasure and gladness.'
Then losing his color, he closed his eyes.
He served Love and in the end is dead from it.
. . . .
May God have mercy on his soul.

Balade [f.84c]

Ch

   Oez les plains du martir amoureus,
   Tous vrays amans, et plourez tendrement!
   De le veoir vueilliez estre songneux
   Et entendre comment piteusement
5 Fait les regrés du grief mal qui l'esprent.
   Se vous povés, faites li brief secours.
   Priés aussi a mains jointes Amours
   Qu'il ait merci de son leal amant,
   Car, par ma foy, veües ses doulours,
10 Il vit sans joye et languist en mourant.

2

   Simple, pali, triste, las, doulereux, [f.84d]
   En souspirant faisant son testament,
   Disant ainsi en la fin de ses geus,
   'Adieu, dame, pour qui muir humblement;
15 Mon cuer vous lay et vous en fay present;
   Autre rien n'ay fors que plaintes et plours;
   Ce sont les biens qu'en la fin de mes jours
   Ay pour amer et estre vray servant.
   Que fait mon cuer a cui Mort vient le cours?
20 "Il vit sans joie et languist en mourant."'

3

   Venez au corps, larmes cheans des yeulx,
   De noir vestu, priant devotement
   Pour l'amoureux, pour le pou eüreux,
   A cui Amours a esté liegement
25 Joie, confort, deduit, esbatement.
   Ses plus grans biens sont plaintes et clamours.
   Et se savoir voulez par aucuns tours
   Comment le las vit sa mort desirant,
   Venez le voir, car certes, sans retours,
30 It vit sans joie et languist en mourant.

15 fors que] forques

38

The Languishing Lover

Listen to the laments of the martyr of Love,
Every true lover, and weep tenderly!
Please be attentive in watching him
And hearing how piteously
He makes complaints for the harsh evils which burn him.
If you can, render him some small aid,
Pray also to Love with hands joined
That he will have mercy on his loyal lover,
For, by my faith, considering his sorrows,
He lives without joy and languishes in dying.

Unhappy, grown pale, sad, miserable, sorrowful,
Making his testament while sighing,
Speaking thus at the end of his pleasures,
'Adieu, lady, for whom I humbly expire;
I leave you my heart and make you a present of it;
I have nothing except laments and tears.
These are the goods that I have at the end of my days
For loving and being a true servant.
What does my heart say, to which Death makes its way?
"He lives without joy and languishes in dying."'

Come to the body, tears falling from your eyes,
Dressed in black, praying devotedly
For the amorous, the seldom happy one,
To whom Love has been absolutely
Joy, comfort, delight, enjoyment.
His greatest goods are laments and mourning,
And if you want to know in some fashion
How the miserable man lives hoping for death,
Come to see him, for surely, with no requital,
He lives without joy and languishes in dying.

Balade [f.84d]

Ch

De ce que j'ay de ma doulour confort,
Du gay ressort qu'en vostre amer reçoy,
De ce que voy que j'ay finé et mort,
Par servir fort, Dangier et son desroy,
5 De ce qu'Ennoy s'est departi de moy,
De ce que n'oy plus plaintes ne doulours,
De Doulx Secours qu'a mes mauls aperçoy,
Grace a ma dame et loenge a Amours.

2

Car long temps ay attendu vie ou mort—
10 Mort par l'accort de dangereux conroy;
Mais par l'ottroy de Mercy, humble et fort,
Et Joie, au port d'un esuillié, conjoi;
Et en l'arroy m'a fait Deduit envoy
Du bien de soy, de la fin de mes plours, [f.85a]
15 Si qu'en ces tours je gariçon conçoi.
Grace a ma dame et loenge a Amours.

3

Vive tous temps a son plaisant deport;
Aie l'apport de souhait par envoy;
Tout esbanoy li soient sans discort,
20 Et le remort d'amer en bonne foy.
Comme je croy son cuer en leal ploy,
Dont en la loy ou prendre je vueil cours
Sans loins sejours, joieusement en doy
Grace a ma dame et loenge a Amours.

1–24 In each stanza the endings of the first six lines are echoed at the end of the following hemistich (confort/ressort). This is 'rime batellée.'
11 Mais] Et; et fort] effort
12 Et] De
15 je] ou

A Lover's Thanksgiving

Because of the comfort I have for my sorrow,
Because of the gay refuge I gain in your love,
Because I see that I have finished off and put to death,
Through valiant service, Danger and his commotion,
Because pain has left me,
Because I no longer have laments and sorrows,
Because of Sweet Help that I gain for my troubles,
Grace to my lady and praise to Love!

For I long awaited life or death—
Death according to Danger's plan.
But by the gift of Mercy, humble and strong,
And of Joy, in the aid of an exile, I am happy.
In his retinue Delight has made me a bearer
Of his goodness, to end my tears,
So that in these events I obtain healing.
Grace to my lady and praise to Love!

May she always live according to her sweet pleasure;
May her wish be fulfilled with quick response;
May all the pleasures be hers without discord,
And the tale of love told in good faith.
Since I believe in her heart loyally,
Therefore, by the law which I wish to follow
Without long delay, joyously I owe for it
Grace to my lady and praise to Love.

Ch

Qui partiroit mon cuer en ij. parmi,
On y verroit l'empriente des beaux yeulx
De ma maistresse, et de ma dame aussi,
Qui de son bien tout le fait valoir mieulx;
5 Et au seurplus, ainsi m'aïde Diex,
Que son doulx vis est en moy si pourtrait
Que quant je pense au gracieux attrait
De ses samblans, que Leauté conjoie,
Il m'est advis que je voie, et de fait,
10 Sourse d'Onnour et riviere de Joie,

2

En tant qu'elle a le corps tel assouvi,
Qu'avoir doit dame au vouloir d'amoureus,
Riant regard, maintien bel et joli,
Fresche coulour, estat riche et joieux,
15 Port d'excellence, et renon gracieux,
Cuer si gentil que Leauté s'i trait,
Et encor plus, chascun qui se retrait
Vers sa biauté, qui les veans resjoie,
Dist, 'Je voy la aussi bien qu'a souhait
20 Sourse d'Onnour, etc.';

3

Si remerci mes yeulx lesquelx ont si
Bien assené que j'en suis eüreux, [f.85b]
Et loe Amours et le povoir de li,
Et ma dame qui puet mes dolereux
25 Maulx alegier, promettant qu'en tous lieux
La serviray encor plus que n'ay fait,
Car c'est de voir—son corps gent et parfait,
Son doulx atour, et sa maniere coie,
Avec Plaisir qui les amans reffait—
30 Sourse d'Onnour et riviere de Joie.

19 qu'a souhait] quassouhait

42

The Image in the Lover's Heart

Whoever would cut my heart in two
Would see there the imprint of the lovely eyes
Of my mistress, who is also my lady,
Who with her goodness increases the worth of all;
And what is more, may God help me,
He would see that her sweet face is so engraved in me
That when I think of the gracious attraction
Of her semblance, in which Loyalty rejoices,
It seems to me that I see, in very truth,
The source of Honor and the river of Joy,

Insomuch as she has a body as perfect
As a lady might have to the desire of the lover,
A laughing look, a fair and pretty manner,
Fresh complexion, high and happy status,
Excellent deportment, and gracious good name,
Heart so noble that Loyalty is drawn to it,
And still further, each person who is attracted
To her beauty, which rejoices the beholders,
Says, 'I see there, as well as one might wish,
The source of Honor and the river of Joy.';

So I thank my eyes, which have so well
Succeeded that I am made happy by them,
And I praise Amour and its power,
And my lady who can assuage
My unhappy afflictions, promising that everywhere
I will serve her still more than I have,
For she is in truth—her noble, perfect body,
Her sweet disposition and quiet manner,
With Pleasure which restores lovers—
The source of Honor and the river of Joy.

APPENDIX

Three Poems in Penn of Related Interest

Two anonymous ballades in Penn have an undoubted relationship to poems of 'Ch' and provide interesting comparison to them. Among other things they suggest that there were informal writing competitions among the poets at court who matched their efforts employing similar subjects and wording. These two works are presented in this appendix together with a third ballade which represents well the droll humor some-times found in poems of the *formes fixes*.

The first work is a ballade whose subject and refrain are close to 'The Castoff Lady' of 'Ch' (V). In his edition of the anonymous ballades Mudge calls the poem's text 'corrupt,' and he merely transcribes it, making no attempt to punctuate. The difficulty of the sense is probably not due so much to a defective text, however, as to a purposeful obscurity and reconditeness on the part of the poet, resembling Provençal *trobar clus*. The poetic exchanges involving Jean de le Mote edited below have this quality, as do certain other lyrics in Penn. Nevertheless, if the specific sense of the poem is in places difficult, we can speak confidently about most of it. The lady who speaks, like the lady of the 'Ch' poem, has been abandoned in her mature years by her lover; she laments in the refrain that he who called loudly upon her when she was young abandons her now that she is older (refrain). Also like the lady of 'Ch', she compares herself to the desolate Dido and Medea, and him to Jason and Aeneas, and she adduces a biblical example. Her reference to him as 'dur Moïses' (l. 1) must refer to Moses' having sent Zipporah back to her father Jethro (Exodus 18). The two-line refrain, characteristic of early Middle French ballades, perhaps indicates composition of this work before the 'Ch' poem. The latter is a more complex and superior work.

The 'annel de la fleur de soucie' (l. 8) which is a cause of the lover's infidelity no doubt refers to the crown of marigolds ('soussie') ascribed to Jealousy in the *Roman de la Rose* (Lecoy, ed., l. 21742). In editing these three poems I have not attempted to emend in order to clarify the meaning.

[MS no. 35]   [The Castoff Lady (2)]

                              Balade   [f.16c]

    Dur Moïses, de langoreuse mort
    M'a Saba morte en Ethyope nee.
    Temps, labours, biens a peu tan est sas tort

44

De toy saoul m'a fait tigre afamee,
5 Qu'au foy ne tiens, mes jus la juste espee;
   Ou se ce non, en moy te justefie.
   Vielle me lais qui jeune m'as hussee
   Pour un annel de la fleur de soucie.

   Ingrast Jason, fleuve de desconfort,
10 Je te plaing plus que ne fovas [fais?] moy, Medee,
   Qu'envers noz dieux n'auras ja tu bon sort,
   E mon labour o ma toison doree.
   Qu'aprés foy m'as povre respudiee;
   Esgarix un sont de menu druerie.
15 Vielle me lais qui jeune m'as hussee
   Pour un annel etc.

   Lasse, Dido, garpie. Sur mon port
   Quel plaint feray de toy, le faint Enee?
   J'ay tout perdu pour t'amour qui m'amort,
20 E de foy faus; or muir desesperee
   Muïre ainsi qui m'as achetivee,
   A qui fornest amant viloterie.
   Vielle me lais qui jeune m'as hussee
   Pour un annel etc.

The second ballade in Penn which matches a poem of 'Ch' (III) is paired with it in the MS, immediately preceding it. The two poems have the refrain, 'Quant ma dame me donna nom d'ami,' and description of the lover's 'day of grace' occupies both. Their rhetorical structures are so similar as to make imitation certain; in each the first stanza attempts to capture the superlative quality of the day, the second describes the action of the day in terms of a personification allegory in which Pity and her helpers defeat Refusal, and the third recapitulates the events and their effects. Again the 'Ch' poem seems an improvement on the other work.

[MS no. 238]   [The Day of Grace (2)]

                          Balade

   S'Amours plaisoit ses tresors defermer
   Pour exaucier un loial amoureux,
   Et Fortune le vouloit confermer
   Estre appellé en ce monde eüreux,
5 Je croy qu'a pou ne porroient ces deux
   Tant l'enrichir, certes, qu'ilz firent my
   Quant ma dame me donna nom d'amy.

   J'estoie avant sans rire ne chanter,
   Triste, pensis, plaintis, et paoureux,
10 Povre d'espoir, sans oser gens hanter,
   Quant Bel Acueil et Franchise le preux,
   Avec Pitié, de Reffus l'orgueilleux
   Me vengerent; mourir par eulx le vy
   Quant ma dame me donna nom d'amy

15 Onques Dangier n'en daigna reculer,
   N'estre vaincu ne post, tant est crueux.

                            45

Je doubtay lors mes amis affoler.
Mercy huchay, jointes mains, tres honteux.
Elle sailli, dont je fus si joieux
20 Qu'en la doulceur de tous biens m'endormy
Quant ma dame me donna nom d'amy.

The third poem, which is presented here as a specimen of humor in Penn congenial to the Middle French lyric mode, is also classed as 'corrupt' by Mudge. In this case the problem probably arises from the author's use of nonce words and a humorous name not otherwise recorded. The poet threatens the lover who does not adhere to proper behavior in love with being devoured by a voracious 'louf,' 'houf,' 'gouf' called 'Cire Miré Bouf.' The nouns probably play on O.F. *lufre* (*louffre*, etc.) and *golafre*, both of which mean *glutton*. It is likely that the appelation of the greedy monster signifies 'Sir Tusked Ox.' Its nature recalls the two fabulous man-eating bovines, Bicorne and Chichevache, known to Chaucer's Clerk, who feed on patient husbands and wives. The ballade counsels service of Amour with humility, generosity, and patience if one is to avoid being eaten and digested ('transglouti') by the perilous beast.

[MS no. 42]   [Sir Tusked Ox]

Balade   [f.18a]

Se tu monde estre veuls en ce monde
Servir t'estuet tresloyaument Amour,
Grace et Bonté, tire Avoir qui maint monde,
Humilité, Attrempence en honnour,
5 Fuir Orgueil, querir Paix et Doulçour.
Perseverer y soit pour le meillour,
Ou estre pues devouré d'un seul louf
Qu'a droit nommé est Cire Miré Bouf.

Se grant avoir ou richesse t'abonde,
10 Pour ce n'en dois avoir plus grant rigour;
Ains plus courtois dois estre que la bonde.
De Fol Cuidier ne te face grevour,
Qu'estre ne dois—trop seroit grant folour.
Or mire dont ton estat et valour,
15 Ou estre pues transglouti d'un seul houf
Qu'a droit nommé est Cire Miré Bouf.

L'amere mort qui tout mort et suronde
Mort un chascun, soit de nuit ou de jour;
Ne sçay comment tant est haute et parfonde.
20 Or t'estuet dont retraire sans sejour
De niceté faire, entiché par errour.
Paciant soies en desroy, sans irour,
Ou peris pues d'un aventureux gouf,
Qu'a droit nommé est Cire Miré Bouf.

PART II

Chaucer and University of
Pennsylvania MS French 15 (Penn)

That the initials 'Ch' stand for Chaucer is an intriguing possibility, but a long shot. The percentages are somewhat better that Chaucer had a hand in some of the 160 or 170 anonymous texts of Penn, whether or not marked with 'Ch', for the collection as a whole and in its parts has a number of notable connections with Chaucer and his circle. That a substantial portion of the texts were gathered together in England in his time is possible, even likely in the light of Oton de Granson's associations with the manuscript.

Expert opinion on the script of Penn agrees in placing its production around 1400, the year of Chaucer's death. The scribes were French.[1] The first leaf has written at the top in a separate hand, 'Droit et ferme,' which is the motto of the kingdom of Bavaria and suggests a connection with Charles VI's queen, Isabelle of Bavaria, whom Charles married in 1385. Noting that the MS contains a substantial number of the poems of Oton de Granson, two with acrostics on 'Isabel,' Charles Mudge would identify Penn with a book of Granson's 'balades' that Isabelle owned in 1401.[2] This is a reasonable suggestion. As I will discuss at the end of Part II, the contents might well have been drawn from Granson's personal collection, whether for a manuscript for Isabel or for another.

In contents Penn is an anthology of fourteenth-century lyrics which seems to have been gathered together with a deliberate aesthetic intention; the anthologist aimed at pleasing variety. He certainly made no attempt to make an inclusive record of any poet's work, or to display one particular form, or to present particular themes or subjects exhaustively. The poems are spread out by author and type with few uninterrupted large blocks. Beyond the 'Ch' initials none of the poets is identified in the rubrics; nevertheless, the authors of 149 of the poems are known from other manuscript sources. Five of the seven authors of these poems have connections with Chaucer. Dominating the center of Penn are 107 works of Guillaume de Machaut, who among fourteenth century French poets exerted by far the most important influence on Chaucer. Flanking and interspersed with Machaut's works in Penn are twenty-seven poems of Oton de Granson, whom Chaucer called the 'flower' of French poets. Eustache Deschamps is represented by at least one poem, and seven more in

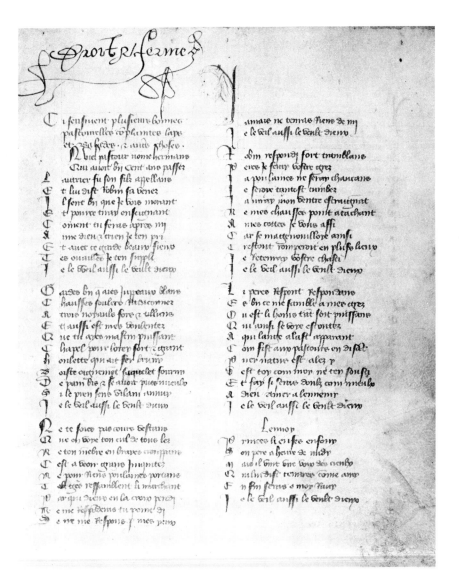

3. The opening folio of University of Pennsylvania MS French 15, showing the motto of Bavaria, 'Droit et ferme,' written at the top in a later hand. There follow below the rubric announcing the contents, 'pastourelles, complaintes, lays, ballades et autres choses'; and the first poem, a pastourelle (without rubric and initial capital).

Penn are probably by him. As with Granson, Deschamps' associations with Chaucer are multiple. Others represented are the musician Grimace, 3 texts; Nicole de Margival, 1 text; Philippe de Vitry, 1; and Jean de le Mote, 1. Nicole and Jean have been seen as influencing Chaucer's work.

Among other groups of poems in Penn are the fifteen 'Ch' works, spread out between texts 235 and 276 and interspersed with the later Granson lyrics. Another distinctive set is formed by the first fifteen poems of the manuscript, all in related five-stanza forms: twelve pastourelles and three 'serventois.' The last thirty-three poems—which follow the last of the Granson, Machaut, and 'Ch' lyrics—form the least interesting group, though not all of these poems are dull.

In order to bring out further the various ways in which Penn is associated with Chaucer, it will be convenient to consider the contents as they pertain to the individual authors. The exchange of poems between Philippe de Vitry and Jean de le Mote provides the freshest and most striking evidence, but its potential relevance to Chaucer is considerably augmented by the fact that Machaut's and Granson's poems dominate the collection. For this reason we will take up their works first.

A. GUILLAUME DE MACHAUT

Machaut's poems are the heart of Penn; they monopolize the center. All 107 that are certainly his are found between poem 72 and 271 of the 310-lyric collection—all but four between 82 and 227.[3] The poems come from all stages and divisions of his work; an analysis suggests that they were selected from one of the full Machaut collections, of which several are extant.

In its order of presentation of Machaut's poems, Penn does not follow in detail the order of any of the collections, but it is by no means a random offering. It seems that the compiler, in selecting the poems, went back and forth within the sections in which the Machaut manuscripts were always divided. Forty of the first forty-seven Machaut poems in Penn comes from his *Louange des dames*, the collective title of his lyrics not set to music.[4] The two lyrics which follow come from a long *dit*, the *Remede de Fortune*.[5] Then forty-six of the next fifty-five are from the lyrics with musical settings, with the other nine of these from the late long poem, the *Voir Dit*.[6] The final three, substantially separated from the others, are from the *Louange*.[7] This summary suggests, and more detailed comparison of the manuscript contents helps to confirm, that the compiler used a collection which began with the *Louange*, followed with the long *dits*, and concluded with the lyrics with musical setting and the *Voir Dit*. Only one of the extant collections conforms to this order, Bibliothèque Nationale français 9221 (E), a late fourteenth-century codex made for the Duke of Berry.[8] One might posit that the exemplar for Penn had common roots with this manuscript. Such association of Penn with the Duke of Berry, even if remote, has interest for this study since Chaucer no doubt became acquainted with this great personage when he was in England for substantial periods of time between 1361 and 1366; the Duke was later to echo a line of Chaucer's in the first line of a ballade that he composed: 'Puiz qu'a Amours suis si gras eschapé' [Since I have escaped from Love so fat].[9]

Though the compiler drew from all sections of the Machaut oeuvre, he did show some partiality in what he included. He selected a much higher proportion of the works set to music than of those without music. Only about a seventh of the *Louange* is represented, but over half of the musical pieces. If one assumes, as seems logical, that the works which had musical settings were more commonly presented than the others, one might surmise that the compiler had become familiar with the Machaut oeuvre particularly in performance, rather than simply from reading, and that he had developed favorites in the process which he included in Penn. This suggests that the compiler was a court figure, instead of a professional scribe or scholar. At the same time, since Penn has a substantial number of non-musical poems, it was evidently not intended to provide texts for musical purposes. The manuscript moreover does not include any of Machaut's motets, always written for musical presentation, which the major Machaut manuscripts included and Chaucer on occasion made use of in his poetry. The motet originally was a religious type, and it remained so in England. Aside from the motets, Machaut's other lyric types are well represented in Penn: forty-two ballades, thirty rondeaux, twenty virelays, seven chants royaux, five lays, and three complaints.

As far as I can determine, there is no significant inclusion or exclusion by the compiler of specific Machaut poems that we know Chaucer used. Scholars have identified Chaucer's uses of thirty-six of Machaut's short poems, and ten of these appear in Penn.[10] Since Penn contains about a fourth of his lyrics, statistical probability is just a little more than satisfied. Nevertheless, since we may well believe that Chaucer was familiar with the whole of Machaut's oeuvre, the fact that his lyrics dominate Penn tends in itself to associate the collection with the English poet.

One point of topical interest. Penn includes Machaut's Sixth Complainte (no. 112), whose opening lines have the acrostic 'Marguerite/Pierre.' This poem evidently was written for Pierre de Lusignan, King of Cyprus, who was Edward III's guest in London in 1363, and whom Chaucer memorializes in the Monk's Tale (ll. 2391–98).[11]

B. OTON DE GRANSON

Granson is well-represented in Penn with a total of twenty-six of his known lyrics, making the manuscript the third largest collection of his poems. All but two of the poems fall into two groups in Penn; one of these groups precedes and the other follows the bulk of Machaut's poems. Sixteen Granson texts fall between Penn nos 18 and 34, and eight between nos 251 and 264.[12] All of the poems are ballades except for six complaints in the first group, including the two with acrostics on Isabel. The first group also includes the sequence of five ballades which Chaucer in part adapted and translated for this triple ballade, 'The Complaint of Venus.' The envoy of the 'Complaint' contains the reference to Granson as 'flour of hem that make in Fraunce,' the only place in his work that Chaucer names a contemporary French poet.

It seems certain that Granson and Chaucer were friends. Granson probably went to England in 1369 after attending the wedding of Lionel of Clarence in Milan; he was in the service of Edward III and Richard II from about that time until 1387, when the death of his father recalled him to Savoy; he returned to

England for an extended stay in 1392–96. Granson shows the inspiration of Chaucer's work in at least two poems: *La Complainte de l'an nouvel*, which makes use of Chaucer's *Book of the Duchess*; and *Le Songe Saint Valentin*, which was inspired by the *Parliament of Fowls*.[13] The first of these Granson works is found in Penn. The two poets also have in common a penchant, not shared by other prominent poets of the century, for St Valentine's Day commemorations.

A significant association of Penn with Chaucer is provided by the text of Granson's ballade sequence. It has some diction and imagery in common with Chaucer's 'Complaint of Venus' that other Granson manuscripts do not share. The rubric is one interesting feature. In Penn the first of the ballades originally bore the rubric 'complainte,' perhaps intended as a title for the group of five though it was later effaced. The other manuscripts identify the poems as ballades, as do the present rubrics in Penn. Charles Mudge suggests that Chaucer's title 'Complaint' originally came from the Granson title that appears in the old rubric.

More certain evidence is provided by the body of the text. As Mudge states, the Penn text of these poems 'is not as corrupt as those of the other two collections and shows a greater affinity to that version used by Chaucer.'[14] The Penn texts of the ballade sequence, with variants from the other manuscripts, and notes on the various relationships to Chaucer's wording, are presented in Appendix A.

C. THE EXCHANGE BETWEEN JEAN DE LE MOTE AND PHILIPPE DE VITRY

Poems nos 62 and 63 of Penn, entitled 'Balade' and 'La Response,' make a fascinating pair, particularly for students of Chaucer. The first poem is an attack by one poet on another, and the second is a rejoinder by the author attacked. The poet of the response is Jean de le Mote, who in 1339 had dedicated his elegy for William of Hainault, *Li Regret Guillaume Comte de Hainault*, to the Count's daughter Philippa, Edward III's queen.[15] The elegy is a likely source for Chaucer. Moreover, the contents of the exchange associate Jean with English court circles and suggest composition in the very years that Chaucer began his service in the courts. The attacking poet is Philippe de Vitry, bishop of Meaux from 1351 to 1361, famous poet-musician and friend of Petrarch. Philippe had such importance in mid-century intellectual life that even a second-hand connection with Chaucer's milieu is significant.

This exchange is little known and less understood. Its significance for the works of the two poets and relevance to Chaucer have not been grasped, largely because scholars have only known them in the garbled versions of a fifteenth-century manuscript, Bibliotheque Nationale fonds latins 3343.[16] The Penn version is much more comprehensible, though by no means without faults and difficulties.[17] In the 'Balade' Philippe accuses Jean of treason to France through his poetic praise of King Arthur; that is, Edward III. In his rejoinder, also a balade, Jean does not deny being in England or writing the poetry, but states firmly that he does not owe allegiance to the French, and that he is serving truth in England. The texts of these two poems which follow are based on Penn, incorporating some readings—set off in brackets—from B. N. Latin 3343 (*B*).

[MS #62]

balade   [f.23b]

De terre en Grec Gaule appellee,
[Castor fuitis fuyans com cers,]
En Albion de flun nommee,
Roys Autheus devenus serfs.
5 Nicement sers
Quant sons fais d'anfent fains amer
D'amour qu'Orpheus ot despite,
Laou tu n'as d'amour fors l'amer,
En Albion de Dieu maldicte.

2

10 T'umbre de fuite yert accusee
Par Radamantus le pervers
Et de roy Minnos condemnee
A vii. tours de queue a revers;
Et a cupers
15 [Contraindra] ta langue a l'aper,
Comme de renoie traïte,
De Flagiton, l'amere mer,
En Albion de Dieu maldite.

3

Certes, Jehan, la fons Cirree   [f.23c]
20 Ne te congnoit, ne li lieux vers
Ou maint la vois Caliopee.
Car amoureus diz fais couvers
De nons divers.
Dont aucuns enfes scet user
25 Com tu, qui ne vaulz une mite
A Pegasus faire voler,
En Albion de Dieu maldite.

1 en] B o
2 C. et polus comme serfs. The references to Castor and to the *river* Albion (l. 3) are puzzling.
4 Roys] B Cers; instead of 'Autheus,' Pognon reads 'Antheus,' which he sees as a version of Acteon.
6 son fais] B soubz fait
7 Orpheus here, I take it, stands as patron and judge of poet-musicians; cf. 'Ch' X, l. 3.
14 Et a cupers] B Eacus pers
15 Contiendra
19 The fountain of Cirrha signifies here the Hippocrene. Cirrha is a town at the foot of Parnassus.
24 enfes] B en fais
26 Pegasus created the fountain of the Muses with his hoof when he first took flight; thus 'Hippocrene.'

Philippe de Vitry

Out of the land called Gaul in Greek,
In flight, like a deer fleeing Castor,
To Albion named for the river,
You have become a serf of King Arthur.
You serve foolishly
When you pretend to love his youthful deeds
With a love that Orpheus finds hateful,
There where you have no love except bitterness,
In Albion cursed by God.

Your shade in flight was accused
By Rhadamanthus the perverse
And condemned by King Minos
With seven turns of his tail backwards;
And with reproaches
He constrained your tongue to loosen
As with a renegade traitor,
At Phlegethon, the bitter sea,
In Albion cursed by God.

Indeed, John, the fountain of Cirrha
Does not know you, nor the green place
Where the voice of Calliope stays.
For you make amorous poems filled
With divers names.
Now any child knows how to write
Like you, who are not able one whit
To make Pegasus fly
In Albion cursed by God.

La Response [f.23c]

O Victriens, mondains dieu d'armonie,
Filz Musicans et per a Orpheus,
Supernasor de la fontaine Helye,
Doctores vrays, en ce pratique Anglus,
5 Plus clers véans et plus agus qu'Argus,
Angles [en chant], cesse en toy le lyon!
Ne fais de moy Hugo s'en Albion
Suis. Onques n'oy ailleurs [vent] ne volee.
Ne je ne sui point de la nacion
10 De terre en Grec Gaulle de Dieu amee.

2

Mais fole atisse, enluminans envie,
Par fauls proces, raportes d'Oleus.
T'a fait brasser buvrage a trop de lie
Sur moy, qui ay de toy fait Zephirus,
15 Car en la fons Cirree est tes escus;
Tous jours l'ay dit sans adulacion.
Or m'as donné a cupers Flangiton,
Fleuve infernal, et les vij. tours d'entree
Sept tourmens sont. Je ne vueil pas tel don
20 De terre en Grec Gaulle de Dieu amee.

3

Contre mal bien servir sers en Albie
Castor, Polus, ne Roys [chiers] Autheus. [f.23d]
Et se li roys Minos enquiert ma vie
Il trouvera Eclo et ses vertus
25 Pour contrester contre Radamiatus
S'il m'acusoit d'aucune traison.
N'ains [nons ne mis en fable n'en] chançon
Qui n'ait servi en aucune contree.
Sy te supplie, ne banny mon bon nom
30 De terre en Grec Gaulle de Dieu amee.

2 per a] B peres
4 pratique] B pratilze
6 Angle cesse
7 For the identity of Hugo, see the discussion below.
8 n'oy] B neus; bout
10 en] B o
11 Eolus here is represented as blowing rumor through the world.
12 raportes] B raporter
22 serfs
27 mis ver ne flabe ne

54

Jean de le Mote

O man of Vitry, worldly god of harmony,
Son of Music and peer of Orpheus,
Greater Naso of the fountain of Helicon,
True doctor, Aulus Gellius in this practice,
More clear-sighted and more acute than Argus,
Angel in song, restrain the lion in you!
Do not make Hugo of me because I am in Albion.
I never had inspiration or flight elsewhere.
And I in no way belong to the nation
Of the land in Greek called Gaul, loved by God.

The report of Eolus always incites foolishly
By false process, inflaming envy.
It has made you brew a drink with too many dregs
For me, who have made of you Zephirus,
For your shield is in the fountain of Cirrha;
I have always said it without flattery.
Now you have given me with reproaches Phlegethon,
The infernal river, and the seven turns upon entering
Are seven torments. I do not wish such a gift
From the land in Greek called Gaul, loved by God.

Serving well against evil I serve in Albion,
Not Castor, Pollux, nor dear King Arthur.
And if King Minos is seeking my life
He will find Echo and her powers
To contest against Rhadamanthus,
If he accuses me of any treason.
I never put a name in fable or song
Which would not have served in any country.
So I entreat you, do not banish my good name
From the land in Greek called Gaul, loved by god.

The 'Balade' is cryptic in detail, but its broad outlines are clear enough. After scornfully accusing Jean of fleeing France and becoming a serf of King Arthur in England, Philippe goes on to describe his prospective punishment in hell and to ridicule his literary endeavors in Edward's service, in particular his use of names in literary allusions. Of Philippe's own literary allusions in his ballade, the most interesting is that to Minos, who condemns Jean's spirit with seven turns of his tail after having constrained him to confess his sins. The notion of a demonic Minos who sentences souls in this bizarre fashion is not found in Vergil; it must originate in Dante's *Inferno*. This allusion to Dante antedates by far any in French poetry previously identified.[18] In Canto V (ll. 1–20) Minos stands outside the second circle, and in sentencing each soul that faces him he entwines his tail about himself as many times as the steps the sinner will have to descend to his punishment. One might expect that Philippe would prescribe nine instead of seven turns of the tail to send the traitor to his proper place at the bottom of hell, but Dante's text invites the discrepancy.[19] By contrast, the reference to Rhadamanthus, who is not named by Dante, originates in the *Aeneid* (VI 566–69). In the third stanza the frame of allusion changes to Ovid. In indicting Jean's verse as uninspired and childish, Philippe refers to the pool of the Muses, and indirectly to the story of its creation by the hoof of Pegasus.[20]

The rejoinder by Jean de le Mote is a dignified attempt to answer the accusations point by point and to placate Philippe at the same time. Jean evidently enjoyed prestige as a poet and musician. Nevertheless, he does not stand on his dignity. In response to Philippe's insults he is self-effacing and diplomatic rather than indignant. He answers the biting attack with praise of Philippe's compositions, and he converts the refrain that presents England as 'cursed by God' into a compliment to France, 'loved by God.' But Jean is not craven. He denies Philippe's accusations forthrightly, alleging that he owes no fealty to France, defending his poetic use of names, and declaring that he will answer Minos' accusations like Echo. He ends with a plea to Philippe not to slander him in France.

It is not certain that in his response Jean evidences a direct familiarity with *Inferno*. His mentioning King Minos and his 'sept tours d'entree' may simply be based on Philippe's words. The reference to Hugo as an example of perfidy, not found in Philippe's poem, appears to be an allusion to Ugolino, famed resident of the circle of traitors (XXXIII.13–78). But coincidentally there is an unidentified Hugo whom Philippe attacks in one of his extant motets; Jean might have known of this Hugo of the motet.[21]

The contents of the two poems indicate that Jean at the time of the exchange is in England, while Philippe is in France. The poems cannot be dated exactly, but there are some very good clues. One is provided in the two-ballade sequel to the Philippe–Jean exchange found in the *B* manuscript; this sequel indeed makes it possible to identify the Jean of Philippe's balade as Jean de le Mote. These ballades appear in Appendix B below. In the first a poet named Jean Campion reaffirms Philippe's criticism of Jean de le Mote, calling him 'Le Mote,' and he makes a reference to Jean's *Parfait du Paon*, which he wrote in 1340.[22] We do not know when Jean died, but Philippe died in 1361, so we know that the exchange took place between 1340 and 1361. The bitterness of Philippe's attack and the conciliatory tone of the rejoinder suggest a time of national dissatisfaction in France and of contentment in England; the years after the great English victories at Crécy and Poitiers (1346 and 1356) seem likely. The latter battle was especially disastrous for France because of King Jean's being taken captive.

Supplying supporting evidence is a motet that Philippe composed which seems to go with his ballade. In the motet he attacks an unnamed writer whom he accuses of feeding the English with the dregs of poetry.[23] The writer under attack is probably Jean again; there are no other likely candidates. The fact that Philippe promises in the motet that France will rise again to put an end to English perfidy also seems to signal a low point in French fortunes, Crécy and Poitiers again. The works that irked Philippe, in which Jean praises Edward's accomplishments, evidently have not survived, though there is a famous Latin motet by John Aleyn that shows what the poetry was like. As Brian Trowell has shown, Aleyn probably composed his motet *Sub Arturo* for 'an unusually magnificent meeting of the Garter Knights at Windsor Castle in 1358, on St George's day.'[24] The guests included the captive King of France, David II of Scotland, the Duke of Blois, and Philippe le Hardi of Burgundy. In founding the Order of the Garter Edward had consciously imitated the Arthurian legend, and for the 1358 celebration 'he finished the Round Tower, to house his Round Table.'[25]

The long stanzas of Jean de le Mote's and Jean Campion's ballades—ten lines of decasyllables—also are characteristic of the 1350's and later, when the metrical form of the ballade was becoming independent of the musical form. In his earlier ballades Jean had used shorter stanzas; the eight ballades intercalated in the *Parfait du Paon*, for instance, have stanzas of from seven to nine lines, with decasyllables found only in two ballades with seven-line stanzas. The other ballades have shorter lines.

The probability that Chaucer read or heard the pair of ballades by Philippe and Jean seems good. They are effective poems, written by well-known authors, which had special topical interest for the English court. The enduring fame of Jean's response is attested to by another circumstance which has special pertinence to Chaucer. As parallel passages show, the poem almost certainly provides the model for the openings of two famous ballades of Deschamps, one addressed to Machaut at his death, and the other a tribute to Chaucer.[26] From the striking correspondences one may infer that the ballade exchange was well known in Deschamps' literary world two or three decades later, and that Deschamps expected the audience of his ballades of praise— including Chaucer—to hear the echoes of the earlier work. The poems, it seems, had become part of a standard corpus of lyrics that most court poets writing in French were familiar with. Because of Jean's connection with England, Deschamps probably knew that Chaucer in particular was ac- quainted with the exchange.

The likelihood that Chaucer knew Jean de le Mote in England, and through him became familiar with the writings and ideas of Philippe de Vitry, makes their life and work of substantial potential relevance to Chaucer. Since the two poets are almost unknown to Chaucer scholarship, it seems desirable to present some of the basic information about each of them, with particular attention to their possible significance to Chaucer's development and career.

1. Jean de le Mote

When or where Jean de le Mote was born is not known. The use of 'le' with the feminine 'Mote' is characteristic of Picard or Walloon, and accords with associations of Jean with Ghent and with the court of Hainault. The first probable extant reference to him dates from 1325–26, occurring in a record of the chancellery of Hainault that shows a payment to 'Jehan de la Mote' for transcribing certain accounts.[27] In 1338 Edward III made a grant of twenty pounds annually to 'John de la Mote of Ghent' for life or until paid an equivalent value.[28] In the next year, 1339, Jean composed the long elegy for William that he dedicated to Queen Philippa.[29] As an earlier scholar has noted, *Li Regret Guillaume* provides a unique contemporary precedent for Chaucer's *Book of the Duchess* in that it presents an elegy in dream vision form. There are also other interesting parallels between the elegies.[30] Particularly because of the occasion of *Li Regret Guillaume*, the death of the Queen's father, Chaucer had good reason for knowing it.

In 1340 Jean wrote two long poems for a patron in Paris, Simon of Lille, goldsmith to King Philip VI. One of these is *Le Parfait du Paon*, a late addition to the cycle of French Alexander romances.[31] The work concerns Alexander's battles in India against King Melidus. Its eight ballades are part of a poetic competition involving Alexander, his generals, and the daughters of Melidus. The other poem is *La Voie d'Enfer et de Paradis*, an extensive allegorical work showing the ways to Hell and to Heaven.[32] This poem is composed in stanzas of twelve octosyllabic lines, while the narrative of *Le Parfait du Paon* is written in Alexandrine laisses, and *Le Regret* Guillaume in octosyllabic couplets except for thirty intercalated ballades.

A reference to Jean by Gilles li Muisis, Abbot of St Martin in Tournay, tells us that Jean was still alive in 1350. In his *Meditations* Gilles lists four men by name who are composers of 'biaus dis.' Jean comes third after Guillaume de Machaut and Philippe de Vitry: 'Now there remains Jean de le Mote, who composes verse and music well, and makes very lovely *dits*, by which many a lord is made joyful, so that he has gained honor and esteem as one of the best authors.'[33] It is notable that Jean is said here to be a composer of music as well as of poetry. No musical settings for his work are extant, but all thirty-eight balades in his long poems might readily be set to music.

It has been suggested to me that Jean's posture in his response is that of a disciple writing to his master. Something like this seems likely. Certainly Jean was not always so polite with his literary brethren as he is in addressing Philippe here. In responding to Campion's insults he explains that as far as he is concerned Philippe is a privileged individual, but Campion is not: 'I don't mind the words of the man of Vitry. I receive his chastening with joy. But you! Go teach shepherds!'[34] If he had spent some of his younger years in Paris with Philippe, either as pupil or devotee, then one may add to his education in the flourishing literary circles of Flanders and Picardy an experience with the intellectual atmosphere of Paris and one of its leading figures. In any event, if Jean was around the royal courts in England in the 1350's and 1360's, he clearly would have been a dominating senior literary personage who could have taught Chaucer much about the contemporary art of poetry.

There seem to remain no records of Jean's later life. No notation of his allowance from Edward is extant after its original bestowal. Perhaps he entered the clergy, a vocation which might explain his statement that he serves against evil, instead of serving Arthur, in England. There is a record from 1361 involving a possible relative of his. An entry in the Calendar of Patent Rolls of Edward mentions a 'knight's fee in Welexham' held by Isabel de la Mote. This may well be the same Isabel de la Mote listed among Queen Philippa's damsels of the chamber in 1337.[35] If she was also a relative of Jean, the possibility of Jean's being associated closely with Chaucer is stronger, since it seems that Geoffrey's wife was also a Hainuyer and damsel to Philippa. Philippa Chaucer, of course, would have been substantially younger than Isabel.[35a]

2. Philippe de Vitry

For a poet as celebrated as Philippe de Vitry was, his surviving work is surprisingly fragmentary. We have his *Ars Nova*, which is a treatise on the isochronic music that he and Machaut helped to bring into vogue, texts of several motets with music, and four minor poems, including the ballade attacking Jean.

Philippe was born in 1291 in one of the six towns in Champagne called Vitry.[36] Like Guillaume de Machaut, his fellow Champenois, he had a career both as cleric and trusted deputy of kings, though he filled even more prestigious posts than Machaut did. He served in various major offices under three French kings, Charles IV, Philippe VI, and Jean II, and he was made Bishop of Meaux in 1351. His connection with Jean II was particularly close; from 1346, four years before Jean became king, he was absorbed in his affairs. He arranged Jean's visit to Clement VI in Avignon in 1350 when Jean had assumed the kingship. In both Paris and Avignon from about 1327 Philippe carried on a friendship with Petrarch, with the two corresponding frequently. Petrarch referred to his friend as 'ever a most keen and ardent seeker after truth,' 'now the foremost poet of France,' 'a most learned man.' Pierre Bersuire, the commentator on Ovid, was another close friend who effusively lauded Philippe.[37]

Among the several later poets who cite Philippe for his poetic and musical creativity is Eustache Deschamps, who twice brackets him with Machaut,[38] especially high praise in the light of Deschamps' relationship to Machaut as protegé and perhaps nephew. Testifying to the endurance of his reputation is a fifteenth-century reference to Philippe by the author of the *Règles de la Seconde Rhétorique*, who credits him with being the originator of the 'maniere' of the motet, ballade, lai, and simple rondeau, as well as a major innovator in music.[39] Philippe is third in this author's list, following Guillaume de Lorris and Jean de Meun, and immediately preceding Machaut, who is presented as the one who settled the lyric forms. Once again we find Phillippe in most distinguished company, credited with high achievement. Though the paucity of surviving texts by him leaves us somewhat in the dark as to the bases of his poetic fame, there is no doubt that in his time he was a highly honored and influential poet.

Jean de le Mote was not the only writer acquainted with Vitry whom Chaucer might have known in his early days at court. Gace de la Buigne, who accompanied Jean II to London in his captivity following Poitiers, was a friend of Vitry's of long standing. In his *Roman des deduis*, a poetic treatise on hunting begun in England, Gace mentions Vitry's power as composer of motets.[40] Nevertheless, as a poet-musician of the popular mode, Jean was more likely than Gace to have been purveyor to Chaucer of the poetic accomplishment and learning of Vitry. It was perhaps as a consequence of Jean's association with Philippe that Chaucer first learned of the two great Italians, Dante and Petrarch. Philippe's reference to the *Inferno* in his ballade suggests good knowledge of the *Commedia*; he might have known Dante personally. Schooled by Philippe's reports, Jean in turn could have relayed information about Dante, and more about Petrarch, to Chaucer. Indeed Jean could have met Petrarch in Paris in Philippe's company. It is curious that Chaucer mentions both Petrarch and Dante by name in more than one poem, while he never mentions Boccaccio despite more obvious opportunities. A reverence for the former two as literary personages, acquired early, might account for the discrepancy in treatment.

More might be said of the specific contents of the Vitry–Mote pair of ballades as they relate to Chaucer's works and to 'Ch's' poems also; for instance, we might consider Vitry's and Campion's comments on Jean's use of proper names in his poetry,[41] and ponder also the nexus of references to the pool of the Muses, which has several correspondences in Chaucer and other poets of the time.[42] However, exploration of such matters promises to supply only small fragments of the evidence needed to ascertain the full part which Jean de la Mote and Philippe de Vitry played in Chaucer's career as poet. We may say confidently that both writers were influential figures in mid-century French poetry, and that Jean had a special relationship to Edward III; thereby, both would have been significant factors in Chaucer's career as poet. While the nature of his particular debt to them remains open to speculation, the presence of the two poems in Penn is most suggestive as regards the time and place of the gathering of materials that went into the manuscript, and as regards the manuscript's association with Chaucer. The most likely time of composition of the exchange is the years after Poitiers, after 1356, when French fortunes were at a low ebb, Edward III was being celebrated as Arthur, and Chaucer had entered court life. It may be that Geoffrey read Philippe's attack soon after it was first communicated to Jean, and that he saw Jean's response shortly after it was composed.

D. Eustache Deschamps

The absence as well as the presence of poems by Deschamps in Penn has significance for our analysis. Only one ballade is surely his, no. 44, the single work in Penn that is found also in the major Deschamps collection, Bibliothè-que Nationale fonds français 840, a huge codex made shortly after his death and devoted exclusively to his writings. MS 840 includes more than fifteen hundred pieces, among them upwards of a thousand ballades; but since Deschamps did not oversee its production it probably does not have all that he wrote, missing in particular works of his earlier years. A likely location of some of his unidentified poems is a manuscript that contains the second largest collection of his known works, B.N.f.fr. nouv. acq. 6221, which is known to be at least half his.[43] Consideration of MS 6221 and its contents, particularly as they overlap with the contents of Penn, is quite suggestive for our purposes here.

Written in the first half of the fifteenth century, MS 6221 is much smaller than MS 840; it comprises 155 pieces, 79 of which appear in MS 840 and may be safely attributed to Deschamps. Of the works in MS 6221, 136 are ballades, 58 of which have envoys—including most of those in the MS known to be by Deschamps.[44] It is among the ballades without envoys, however, that Penn has important correspondences with MS 6221. Penn has fourteen ballades also contained in MS 6221; in the latter these are found in two discrete ballade series.[45] The first series has ten ballades, MS 6221 nos 33 to 42, six of which Penn also contains. Of the ten, two appear in MS 840 and are therefore known to be by Deschamps. The light moralizing tone and didactic subject matter common to works in this group make it likely that he was the author of all, and thus of the six poems in Penn.[46] If he wrote them, it no doubt was early in his career since nine of the ten lack envoys (including the two which are surely his). Deschamps pioneered and popularized the use of envoys with ballades, but he would not have employed them as a usual thing until after Machaut's death in 1377.[47] The time of composition and collection into a group of these ten ballades would be the 1360's and early 1370's when Deschamps (b. 1345) was learning the poet's art.

The second series of ballades in MS 6221 which contains works of Penn is longer, comprising the 29 pieces from no. 82 to 110. In this group there are no envoys, nor are there works found in the Deschamps MS 840. The subject matter and treatment are not typical of Deschamps unlyrical style, and indeed eight of the poems are known to be by Guillaume de Machaut. All 29 works of the series are love lyrics that resemble in tone the bulk of Machaut's work.[48] Eight poems found in Penn appear in this series, five of them by Machaut. Though the remainder of MS 6221 is largely Deschamps' or attributable to him, none of the 29 poems probably are his. Placed as they are in the center of the MS, they provide a nucleus of standard works around which to gather his lyrics. One is reminded of Penn, in which the Machaut poems also occupy the center, surrounded by lyrics of Granson, 'Ch', and Deschamps.

The poems which Penn has in common with MS 6221 are scattered through its first three-quarters. Its associations with the two series of poems in MS 6221 suggest that the Penn collection was being assembled in the same years that those two series were taking shape, before or around 1370. They also suggest that some of the same people had a hand in originating parts of the two collections. These may well have been literary people associated with King Jean of France and his sons, whom Chaucer and his associates would have come to know from their recurrent presence in England after Jean's capture at Poitiers in 1356 until his death in London in 1364.

E. Jean Froissart and the Pastourelle Section

Considering the substantial diffusion of the works of other fourteenth-century poets, it is remarkable that no poems known to be by Jean Froissart exist outside the large collections devoted to his poetry, MSS B.N.f.fr. 830 and 831. Like all the other anthologies, Penn has no identified poems of his; however, the set of fifteen poems which opens the MS, twelve pastourelles and three serventois, has significant associations with Froissart's poetry. The works all seem to have been composed in his home territory prior to 1370, and the form and subject matter of several of the pastourelles present unique correspondences among extant texts with Froissart's twenty pastourelles.[49]

The fifteen poems, which we may call the pastourelle section, make up the most distinctive group in Penn, and they seem somewhat obtrusive placed at the head of the MS. In the remainder of Penn there is a consistent and tasteful alternation of standard court forms—especially ballade, rondeau, and virelay—but before we arrive at these there come seriatim the fifteen rather long lyrics with virtually the same metrical form, of types typical of the puy more than the court.[50] Furthermore, in matters of dialect these are the most distinctive works of any in the MS. The language accords with the numerous place names in the texts in identifying them as provincial productions from the Picard dialect area. All of this is to say that the pastourelle section provides a clearly-defined introduction to the anthology, but not that it is inappropriate. Like the bulk of the MS, it is made up of valuable and interesting poems; the works have an appealing local realism which in certain of them blends into intriguing fantasy; their predominant didactic and historical subject matter imparts moral seriousness to the collection at the outset; and there is sufficient reference to the subject of love and use of literary allusion to foreshadow these major elements in the body of Penn. It is quite possible to see the pastourelle section as a well thought-out opening to the anthology.

Froissart's known poems include several chants royaux whose rubrics inform us that they were crowned in the puys of Lille, Abbeville, and Valenciennes. It is clear, then, that he frequented the puys in and around his home territory of Hainault. Nevertheless, despite the fact that the pastourelle was a puy form, Froissart's compositions of the type were written on court subjects, evidently for court audiences. It seems that in his pastourelles he was attempting to adapt the genre to the mode of the nobility, and to standardize it as a *forme fixe*. Judging by the absence of imitations, he had little success in the attempt, though his own pastourelles are good poems. Their chief distinctive features are exceptionally long stanzas of octosyllabic lines, and the use of historical and occasional subjects. Some of the Pennsylvania pastourelles, especially two written just before Froissart began composing in the form, display the same characteristics, though they do not have the marks of court poems. The two pastourelles have stanzas of fifteen and sixteen octosyllabic lines, and feature dialogues of shepherds in which events of the Hundred Years War figure prominently.[51] They thereby are related to Froissart's *Chronicles* as well as to his pastourelles.

This group of poems might well have been carried to England and become well-known there. From the time that the future Edward III visited Hainault with his mother in 1326 and became engaged to Count William's daughter Philippa, until the end of Edward's reign in 1377, England's ties to the Picard dialect area were particularly strong, with a substantial infiltration of English court circles by people from that area; Jean de le Mote, Froissart, and Chaucer's wife are three examples. It is possible that one of the Hainuyers or Picards who came to London in these times carried with him the pastourelle section, as a whole or in parts. Froissart in particular might have done so.

F. Nicole de Margival

Sometime before 1328, probably around 1310, Nicole de Margival composed a long dream poem, *Le Dit de la Panthère d'Amours*,[52] in which he inserted nineteen lyrics of his own, Adam de la Halle, and others. The seventeenth of these is a rondeau of his, 'Soyez lie et menez joye,' which his lady sings to the lover when—in his imagination—she grants him her love. This lyric appears separately in Penn (no. 202) as well as in two musical repertory MSS. Its presence in Penn supports our notion of the MS as a collection of lyrics from early and mid-century. No doubt it is one of the earliest in time of composition, and the fact that it is placed well past the mid-point of the MS confirms other indications that no rigid principle of chronology was at work in the formation of the collection.

The presence of the rondel adds to the potential connections of Penn with Chaucer. A relationship between Chaucer's *House of Fame* and *La Panthère d'Amours* has been suggested by several scholars, and on the basis of similarities in plot structure I am inclined to agree that there is a connection.[53] Though the rondeau in Penn has thoroughly conventional diction, so that in itself it offers no significant precedent for Chaucer's work, its presence does suggest that the anthologist of Penn could have known *La Panthère d'Amours*, as Chaucer probably did, from a MS in England.

G. Grimace

The only other poet whose known works are represented in Penn is identified simply as 'Grimace' in the musical repertory MSS which contain his works.[54] Five of his poems are known, and texts of three of these, all rhyme royal ballades, are in Penn. The origins of the other MSS suggest that Grimace worked in the courts of south France; the music suggests that he was contemporary with Machaut, writing before mid-century. Gilbert Reaney speculates that the double ballade, 'Se Zephirus, Phebus et leur lignie'/'Si Jupiter, qui par grant melodie' (nos 190 and 191) might have been composed for Counts Gaston Phebus of Foix and John I of Aragon. The presence of the works of Grimace reinforce the early-century associations of the Penn anthology and confirm its broad eclecticism. Travel between England and southern France in the fourteenth century, of course, was common.

H. Lyric Types and Metrical Forms in Penn

Even though one has to be content with a relatively scant return for the amount of data considered, and has to settle for probabilities rather than certainties, analysis of the contents of Penn according to the frequency and distribution of metrical types is a good source of information on the MS.

In considering the basic makeup of Penn, one may begin with the assumption that MSS of Machaut's work—the impressive codices of the most influential Middle French poet—provided the major exemplars for the subsequent fourteenth-century collections of lyrics. In their presentation of the various lyric types all of the comprehensive Machaut collections offered two differing models. One of these was supplied by the section known as the *Louange des Dames*, made up of his lyrics not set to music, some 282 works ultimately. In the *Louange* variety is the organizing principle, with the types intentionally mixed and alternated. Ballades dominate, 207 of them providing nearly three-quarters of the total. However, the series of ballades are invariably brief, being frequently interrupted by single specimens of the 60 rondeaux, 7 chants royaux, and 7 virelays.

63

By contrast, the other model which the Machaut MSS supplied dictates a careful segregation of types; the lyrics set to music are always rigidly divided, with a section devoted to the lays followed by separate groups of motets, ballades, rondeaux, and virelays. With the Machaut poems set to music the ballades are numerically less dominant than in the *Louange*, their total of 45 comprising little more than a fourth of the whole number. Each of the other types has substantial representation.

The MSS of the non-musician poets of the next generation followed one or the other of the two Machaut models. Froissart's lyrics are strictly separated by type: lay, pastourelle, chant royal, ballade, virelay, and rondeau. The same in general holds for the great Deschamps collection, except only that the rondeaux are intermixed with virelays (apparently reflecting the near kinship of the forms). On the other hand, Granson's collections follow the model of the *Louange*. The largest group of Granson lyrics, that found in the Neuchatel MS, is like a smaller version of the *Louange*. The 59 ballades, making up 76 percent of the total of 77 poems, are spaced out by a scattering of 8 rondeaux, 1 virelay, 8 complaints and related types, and 1 lay.

Penn, too, follows the model of the *Louange* in the intermingling of types, but the ballade is less dominant in it. Penn has very near the proportions of the total Machaut lyric production, though it includes no motets. Machaut's ballades make up about 57 percent of the sum of his lyrics, while the 108 ballades of Penn comprise 54 percent of its 310 poems. Besides the ballades, Penn contains 55 rondeaux, 38 virelays, 28 five-stanza works (13 pastourelles, 12 chants royaux, and 3 serventois), 12 complaints and related types, and 9 lays. Ballades are distributed through most of Penn. After the opening pastourelle section, series of ballades are interrupted regularly by lays or complaints, and subsequently by an increasing number of rondeaux (after no. 81) and virelays (after no. 121), and a few chants royaux (after no. 93).

If we consider the metrics within the various lyric types we find that the varieties of ballades and rondeaux represented in Penn have significance. Numerically the most popular metrical form in the MS is Machaut's favorite in his works, the rhyme royal ballade, found in 63 poems (including in Penn, 18 by Machaut, 5 Deschamps, 3 Grimace). There are 25 of his second favorite, the ballade with eight-line ababccdD stanzas (including 17 by Machaut, 1 by Granson); and 36 of Granson's most favored form, the ballade with eight-line ababbcbC stanzas (including 7 by Granson, 4 Machaut, 1 'Ch').[55] The ballade with stanzas of ten lines, ababbccdcD, the usual form of 'Ch', is represented in Penn by 19 poems (including 8 'Ch', 3 Granson, and 1 Jean de la Mote). No other ballade forms are particularly important; the remaining 25 ballades are in 16 verse forms.

As mentioned more than once, the use of envoy is indicative of the dating of ballades. Since the musical form of the ballade did not accomodate an envoy, it was only in the last quarter of the fourteenth century with the rise of the non-musicians that ballade envoys came into vogue. Only 11 of the Penn ballades have them, all but one of these appearing among the last 82 texts. There is perhaps a good reason for the early appearance of the one. It is poem no. 20 and the only Granson ballade in Penn which has an envoy. Two matters indicate that it was designed as an introductory piece. In the first place, in its substance it seems like one. It opens with the poet offering a 'Salut de paix' to all lovers; he goes on to provide a general statement about the life of love, offering disdain to the ill-natured ones. In the second place, it is placed at the head of the Paris collection of Granson poems (B.N.f.fr. 2201), long before any other ballades with envoy. In Penn—comparably, though not so ostensibly—it is the first of a series of 15 Granson works. One might guess that Granson composed it late for use as an introduction.[56]

The other ballades with envoys are nos. 229, 230, 267, 279, 281, 288, 296, 298, 303, and 309. None of the group seems to have attained any circulation, for none appear in any other extant MS. The lack of envoys in the ballades through a large part of Penn indicates a date before 1375 for most of the poems in that section; if even a few were composed later, we would expect some ballade envoys. At the same time, the presence of envoys among the later ballades suggests a later date for a substantial proportion of that part. That all poems there are not late, however, is shown by the appearance of early Machaut lyrics as far along as nos 269–71. Moreover, the 7 ballades of Granson that appear among nos 251–64 are probably earlier poems of his.[57] With the poems of 'Ch' too, which appear between texts nos 235 and 276, no matter of form suggests late composition.

The forms of the rondeaux of Penn seem to confirm that the later works in time of composition tend to appear in the later part of the MS, but that not all in that part are late. Of the 55 rondeaux, 33 are in the early eight-line form that Machaut and Froissart used almost exclusively, and 17 are in the sixteen-line form that Granson and later poets favored.[58] It is an interesting complication, though, that one of the 16-line rondeaux was composed by the earliest known poet represented in the MS, Nicole de Margival.[59] The eight-line specimens, 26 of 33 composed by Machaut, all appear in Penn before poem no. 210 except for the single 'Ch' rondeau (no. 260); at the same time, except for Nicole's poem (no. 202), the sixteen-line rondeaux—all anonymous—appear from no. 214 on.

We might briefly note the associations of the 'Ch' works with other poems of Penn in matters of versification. Among the five-stanza poems of Penn, the four chants royaux most resemble the seven Machaut chants. Unlike the pastourelles, they lack refrain, are uniformly decasyllabic, and have no stanzas longer than twelve lines. All of the five-stanza works in Penn seem relatively early. As for the ballades of 'Ch', as the analysis above shows, he shares with Granson, Jean de le Mote, and some anonymous poets the ten-line ballade stanza. Only 'Ch' and Granson are represented by the twelve-line ababb-ccddedE ballade stanza (one each). The one ballade of 'Ch' with an eight-line stanza is in the favored form of Granson, ababbcbC. In Penn, then, his rondeaux and chants associate 'Ch' with Machaut, his ballades with Granson in particular.

There are also matters of some interest in the relationships one may find of Penn with the organization of the Chaucer MSS and the versification of his English works, but most of these are not distinctive enough to warrant comment here. It is perhaps worth remarking that Penn and Chaucer both follow Machaut in making rhyme royal the most favored stanza, and that the second most common stanza in both Penn and Chaucer's work, the Monk's Tale rhyme (ababcdcd), happens to be the one most used by Froissart and Granson, as well as favored by Deschamps.[60] In his English works Chaucer does not employ the 10-line stanza that 'Ch' most uses, and which is also well represented in the poems of Froissart, Deschamps, and Granson. Only two of the rondeaux in Penn follow the rhyme scheme of Chaucer's four specimens in *Parliament of Fowls* and 'Merciles Beaute.'

CONCLUSION: GRANSON AS POSSIBLE ANTHOLOGIST OF PENN

The suggestion of Charles Mudge, mentioned earlier, that Penn is 'le livre des Balades Messire Othes de Grantson' which belonged to Isabelle of Bavaria and for which in 1401 she had made two golden clasps, is quite reasonable though by no means inevitable.[61] Penn is well written but it is not an obvious royal display piece, having no illuminations. As for its identification as a book of Granson's works, even if we attribute a substantial number of the anonymous works to Granson, Machaut would remain the dominant poet of the collection. Of course, if Granson had personally ordered the MS to be made for Queen Isabelle, the attribution of the whole to him would be quite natural. And if he had dedicated (or rather re-dedicated) the Isabelle poems to her, her contentment with an unilluminated codex would be understandable—the texts themselves would possess the main personal interest.

What is particularly appealing about the theory is that everything we know of the Penn collection seems to fit in with the idea that Granson was the anthologist: the dominance of Machaut, the various other poets represented, the forms represented, and the careful organization. The theory provides a sound basis for suggesting how these particular lyrics came to be organized in the MS in the way we find them. In this conclusion, then, I will briefly outline how the MS might have come into existence, beginning with some facts about Granson.

Granson's dates (c. 1340–97) roughly parallel Chaucer's. His acquaintanceship with men of the English court perhaps began in Savoy in 1362.[62] In 1368 he probably accompanied the wedding party of Lionel of Clarence from Savoy to Milan, and he may well have stayed with the same group on their return to London in 1369. In any event he set sail from London in 1372 with the Earl of Pembroke, and in the ensuing English naval defeat he was captured by the Spanish and held until 1374. On his release Granson returned to England and he remained in the service of John of Gaunt and the English kings until 1386 when his father died. From 1392 to 1396 he was back in England for substantial periods of time.

From 1369 until his death in 1397, then, England was the primary center of Granson's activities, though he spent substantial periods in his home Savoy, and he travelled around Europe on military and diplomatic missions, developing his contacts especially with the French royal court—a connection which may be substantially documented.[63] All indications are that Granson began writing poetry early, and that it was an important avocation for him throughout his life. The Barcelona MS contains twelve works that he in all likelihood wrote before his release by the Spanish in 1374.[64] Eight of these are found in Penn, including the 'Cinq ballades ensievans,' which are the source for Chaucer's 'Complaint of Venus,' and 'La Complainte de l'an nouvel,' inspired by the *Book of the Duchess*. Some of the other works seem even earlier, while

Granson's rondeaux and ballades with envoys no doubt come substantially later.

With these few facts as background we may postulate the process of gathering the texts which later were to make up Penn. Since Guilluame de Machaut was by far the strongest influence on Granson throughout his career, Granson probably brought a large number of Machaut texts gathered from a full MS with him to England in 1369. If not, he would have found comparable collections and a full MS or two in England, some a legacy of the extended forced visits of Jean II and his sons. The Machaut texts were to form the nucleus of Penn. In the years from 1369 to 1386, Granson would bring other sets of poems into his personal collection, both works found in England and picked up in his travels. Among these well might have been (1) a set of Picard pastourelles brought across the Channel by Hainuyer associates of Queen Philippa; (2) the ballade exchange between Philippe de Vitry and Jean de le Mote (Jean's answer obviously composed in England), along with several poems probably written in England filled with the more or less obscure classical reference characteristic of Jean (such as Penn nos 16, 19, 35); (3) a set of works not set to music, mostly ballades, which had achieved some currency and would later appear in collections like B.N.f.fr. 6221, Westminster Abbey 21, and the *Jardin de Plaisance*; (4) a group of texts of lyrics set to music, including some ballades of Grimace, one or more poems of Nicole de Margival, and a good number of virelays and eight-line rondels; (5) some lyrics of his London court friend 'Ch' which had probably been composed before Granson arrived in England.

When Granson returned to Savoy in 1386 to claim his inheritance, he would have carried this accumulation of lyrics with him. If some time in the following years he decided to have a book made for Queen Isabelle, he assembled the works for a scribe, indicating with considerable care the order in which he desired them to be placed. Toward the beginning, almost directly after the introductory pastourelles, he placed a set of his own works, which he followed with a good number of the better-known lyrics of other poets, including especially works from Machaut's *Louange*. After text no. 114, all the way to no. 227, Machaut's works that are elsewhere set to music dominate; mixed in with these are a substantial number of rondeaux, virelays, and ballades by other poets which probably had also been set to music. After no. 227 to the end Granson had put in mainly works not designed for musical accompaniment. Among these are another set of Granson's works, the 'Ch' poems, and three Machaut ballades from the *Louange*. In this final section are also increasingly found lyrics which may not have been part of the collection Granson brought from England. The form and content being in the later Granson manner, the works probably were composed in France by Granson and by poetic disciples of his, poets of less originality and merit than those represented earlier in the collection. After no. 276, the last of the 'Ch' poems, the MS is made up exclusively of such works. But even using these later poems to complete the MS, the hundred folios provided in the codex were not quite filled. The last eight were left blank. The scribe indeed may have been interrupted in his work on the last pages in Penn when Granson was tragically killed in a duel in Savoy in 1397.

Lacking a full report by contemporaries, we can only attempt to reconstruct history on the basis of the information that we have. The foregoing reconstruction, which fits very well the many facts we can derive from the contents of Penn, has at least enough of truth in it to provide suggestive insight into the process of composing, collecting, and disseminating the French court lyric in the time that Chaucer was deeply involved in this literary enterprise. Such insight we can get no place else.

APPENDIX A

Granson's Five Ballades

The text of the ballade sequence of Granson which is the basis of Chaucer's 'Complaint of Venus' has not been available in anything close to a full edition. Arthur Piaget, whose edition of Granson's poetry is standard, edits only the Paris MS (B), sometimes emending silently with Neuchâtel (A); Ludwig Schirer also edits B; and Amadée Pagès edits the strange Barcelona text (C), noting variants from B.[1]

As it happens, Penn has the best of the texts and the nearest to Chaucer's model. Only B and Penn present the five poems in sequence in the order which Chaucer obviously had before him; in the other two MSS the texts are separated and the order is mixed.[2] MS B treats the poems as a unit, using one rubric, 'Les cinq balades ensievans,' while in Penn each poem is headed up 'Balade.' However, as Charles Mudge noticed, the first of the poems in Penn originally had the rubric 'Complaint,' which he reasonably surmised was intended as a title for all five poems and perhaps was the source of the word 'Complaint' in the traditional title of Chaucer's work.[3]

MS C presents the worst of the texts, its orthography and some grammatical forms reflecting its Catalan origins. Though it does retain many of the better readings, numerous passages in it are completely different from the other MSS and for the most part clearly inferior to them. In the edition I have limited the record of variant readings of C to those in which the sense is affected; nevertheless, C shows more variants than A and B together, which I have more fully recorded.

The text of B is not bad, but it is quite imperfect. It lacks the third stanza of Ballade II; as a result of omissions and added words, eight of its lines have too many or too few syllables (I 5, 14; II 9; IV 2; V 6, 7, 9, 19); and three readings are inferior or mistaken (I 15; II 5; V 4). While MS A breaks up the five-ballade unit, the detail of its text is better than that of B. Though the scribe muddles three readings (III 15, 17; IV 3), only two lines are mismetered (II 10, 18). Penn both retains the complete unit and has a very good text. In it also only two lines have imperfect meter (II 15; V 19), and the text makes good sense throughout except at the beginning of Ballade V, when the scribe seems to have become confused about the meaning and put verbs in the second and third person when they should be in the first (ll. 1, 3).

In the envoy of his triple ballade, 'Complaint of Venus,' Chaucer states that he is translating Granson 'word by word,' which is an exaggeration. Only parts of his work can be called a translation; the whole rather is an adaption of the first, fourth, and fifth of Granson's ballade series. Chaucer no doubt chose the best and liveliest poems of the five. He changes the point of view from Granson's male narrator to a female narrator. The change suggests that he had a specific occasional purpose for the composition. As

69

might be expected, the variant readings which bear on Chaucer's translation are few. In the notes I have presented all of Chaucer's lines in which variants might have significance, but I will discuss here only those with reasonably clear implications about Chaucer's Granson text.

In attempting to ascertain which MS is closest to Chaucer's original we may dismiss C from consideration. If Granson wrote the group of balades while he was in captivity in Spain, which is not improbable, the text of C may be directly related to Granson's earliest version of the work; nevertheless, it has no unique readings suggestive of Chaucer's language, and—as an inspection of the recorded variants will verify—there are a good number which destroy or impair the similarities.

Penn no doubt is the closest to Chaucer's original. The confusion in verbs at the opening of its Ballade V obviously impairs the parallel at that point, but this is the only place in Penn where the other MSS of the balades are clearly closer to Chaucer's reading. More indicative than the scribal blunder here are competing readings of Penn, A, and B which make equally sound sense. In these the Penn version is consistently closer to Chaucer. Thus, in Ballade I 5, the A MS speaks of 'ses doulz fais, ses maintiens,' instead of 'ses doulz fais feminins' as in B and Penn. Though both make sense, it is clear that Chaucer's noun 'manhood' in his corresponding line was suggested by 'feminins' (adjusting to the change in point of view). In Ballade IV 18, similarly, MS A has 'encombreux a passer' instead of 'a user' of B and Penn which Chaucer's 'the usyng' echoes. In IV 2, A has 'faciez bien comparer' and B 'faciez comparer,' while Penn presents 'faciez cher comparer,' which is the obvious source of Chaucer's 'ful dere abye.' In the same poem, Chaucer's colorful 'Jalousie be hanged be a cable' seems a more likely counterpart of 'Jalousie, c'est la mere du déable' of A and Penn than the weaker 'l'amer [bitterness] du déable' of B.

In Ballade V Penn has three readings closer to 'Complaint of Venus' than A and B. An interesting transformation is Chaucer's change of 'de tous les liex eslire' (l. 11, Penn) into 'Chese the best that ever on erthe went,' which preserves the geographical image of 'liex' ('places'), which is not at all present in 'de tous les bons' of B and 'biens' of C. In V 13, 'aime . . . si fort que' of Penn is not only clearly superior to 'ainsi que' of A and B, but it is also closer to Chaucer's 'love well . . . never stente.' Likewise the flat 'ce que choisi as' of B in V 18 is not suggestive of Chaucer's intensive 'so high a grace,' as 'si bien que' is in A and Penn.

There is no question that Penn offers the best text of Granson's series as a whole and that nearest to Chaucer's model. In the following edition I have presented the Penn text unaltered throughout except for capitalization, punctuation, and expansion of abbreviations.

[I; MS #30]

Balade

[f.15c]

    Il n'est confort qui tant de bien me face
    Quant je ne puis a ma dame parler
    Comme d'avoir temps, loizir, et espace
    De longuement en sa valour penser
5 Et ses doulz fais femenins recorder
    Dedens mon cuer, c'est ma vie par m'ame,
    Ne je ne truis nul homme qui m'en blasme,
    Car chascun a joye de li loer.

    Il a en lui beauté, bonté, et grace
                                         [f.15d]
10 Plus que nulz homs ne saroit deviser:
    C'est grant eür quant en si po despace

Dieu a voulu tous les biens assambler;
Honneur la veult sur toutes honnorer;
Onques ne vy si plaisant jeune dame
15 De toutes gens avoir si noble fame,
Car chascun etc.

Ou qu'elle soit bien fait et mal efface;
Moult bien li siet le rire et le jouer;
Son cuer esbat et les autres solace
20 Si liement qu'on ne le doit blasmer;
De li veoir ne se puet nulz lasser;
Son regart vault tous les biens d'un royaume;
Il samble bien qu'elle est tresnoble femme,
Car chascun etc.

Rubric Penn Complainte *neatly removed and* Balade *written over it. Rubricator's instruction in margin,*
Complainte. *A* Balade amoureuse, *B* Les cinq balades ensievans, *C* Autra [Balada]—1 *B* biens—3
C Commant—5 *B* Et de ses doulz, *C* Ne ses, *A* fais ses maintiens r.—7 *C* Et crois nul, *B* me b.—8
AB lui—9 *B* li bonte beaute—11 *B* pou de place, *C* pou desplace—12 *A* tant de b.—13 *C* le
vuet—14 *B* jeune *missing*—15 *B* femme—17 *C* fet o maul—18 *A* lui, et *missing*, *C* Tres ben le rier e
le—19 *A* soulaces, *C* soulassa—20 *C* Si sagement, *A* lui scet, *BC* len doit—21 *A* lui, *C* nulh ne sen
doit l.—23 *C* tres bonna, *A* fame
    Parallel lines in Chaucer's 'Complaint of Venus' (line nos. in parentheses) for which variants in
Granson's poem have possible significance. Particular words in question are italicized. Lines are
keyed to Granson line nos.
1 Ther nys so high *comfort* to my pleasaunce (1)
3 *As* for to have leyser of remembraunce (3)
5 Upon the *manhood* and the worthynesse (5)
7 Ther oghte *blame me* no creature (7)
9 In him is *bounte*, wysdom, governance (9)

[II; MS #31]

Balade

A mon advis Dieu, Raison, et Nature
En lui fourmer se sont bien entendus,
Car faite l'ont de tous les vices pure
Et paree de toutes les vertus.
5 Ne je ne croy qu'au jour d'ui vive nulz
C'onques veïst dame miex assevie;
Se n'est pourtant que d'amer n'a envie,
Car trop par est son cuer plain de reffus.

Le vis a bel, fassonné a droiture,
10 Le plus doulcet qui onques fust veüx;
Col, main, et bras, couleur, et cheveleure
De tous les beaux sont les plus beaux tenus;
Corps gracieux, mignotement vestus,
Chantant, dansant, et de maniere lie,
15 Mais son temps pert qui d'Amours la prie   [f.16a]
Car trop etc.

Loyauté, sens, honneur, et nourreture,
Et doulz maintien sont d'elle congneüs;
Tresbien entent et respont par mesure;
20 De tous les biens est son cuer pourveüx;

Le dieu d'Amours ne deveroit querir plus
Si li prenoit talent d'avoir amie,
Et si croy je que ceste n'aroit mie
Car trop etc.

Rubric A Balade amoureuse, *C* Autra [Balada]—2 *A* A lui . . . estandus—5 *C* Et je, *A* croy au—6 *A* Qui onques, *C* Home qui vist d.—7 *C* Si mes pourquant damour ma enamie—*Stanzas 2 and 3 inverted in C*—8 *B* et a d., *C* pour d.—10 *A* o. mais f.—11 *C* cou elh mens b.—12 *C* les biens . . . pus biens—13 *C* Cuers g. muyt netament—14 *B* Dansant chantant et de chiere lie—15 *AC* p. cilz qui damer, *B* p. cil—17–24 *missing in B*—17 *C* Honour et sans bieute et—18 *B* delle bien c.—21 *A* devroit—23 *A* Sil lui, *C* Si le

[III; MS #32]

Balade

Or est ainsi que pour la bonne et belle,
Gracieuse, ou tous biens sont manans,
Je sui ferus ou cuer soubz la mamelle
Du dart d'Amours dont le fer est trenchans.
5   Et si vous dy qu'il a passé vii. ans,
Mais encor n'est la playe refermee,
Car sans mercy ne peust estre sanee.
Priez pour moy, tous les loyaulx amans.

Helas! Pitié, tresdoulce damoiselle,
10 Je vous en prie que me soiez aidans.
Contre Dangier soustenez ma querelle,
Car il est fort et ses amis sont grans,
Durté me hait et Paour m'est nuisans.
Se par vous n'est ma santé recouvree
15 Pour Bien Amer yert ma vie finee.
Priez pour moy etc.

De Bien Amer tous les jours renouvelle
Le cuer de moy qui est obeissans
En attendant le bon plaisir de celle
20 A qui je sui et vueil estre servans.   [16b]
Las! Je ne sui que simples et souffrans,
Et me soustien sur ma loyal pensee
Jusques Mercy m'ait sa grace monstree.
Priez etc.

Rubric A Balade amoureuse, *C* Autra [Balada]—1 *B* bonne b., *C* que par—2 *C* en tous—3 *C* Suy je, *AB* suis—4 *C* Dun dart—5 *A* grant temps, *C* gran tamps—6 *C* Quencer non es, *A* ressanee—7 *A* Et s., *C* Qui s. *Stanzas 2 and 3 inverted in C*—9 *C* Et las—10 *AB* vous prie, *C* moy sovas—12 *C* ilh sont fours—13 *C* Dubte me fet e pasor—14 *C* Qui par—15 *C* Qui sans merci no—*A* et ma, *B* est . . . fine—17 *C* chascus jours, *A* renenouvelle—18 *C* Lamour . . . qui soy, *B* obeissant—19 *C* Pour atandans le dous—20 *C* De qui, *AB* suis—21 *AB* suis—22 *C* Je me . . . sus me l., *AB* soustiens—23 *C* mot sa

The reading in Penn and B of line 5, 'vii. ans,' specifying the period the lover's wound has been open, recalls the 'eight yeer' sickness of Chaucer's narrator, also uncured, in Chaucer's *Book of the Duchess*, ll. 36–38. If there is a relationship, Granson would be the imitator.

Balade

Certes, Amour, c'est chose convenable
Que vos grans bien faciez cher comparer,
Veillier ou lit et jeuner a la table,
Rire en plorant et en plaignant chanter,
5   Baissier les yeulx quant on voit regarder,
Souvent changier couleur et contenance,
Plaindre en dormant et songier a la dance.
Tout a rebours de ce qu'on veult trouver.

Jalousie, c'est la mere du déable,
10 Elle veult tout vëoir et escouter,
Ne nulz ne fait chose si raisonnable
Que tout a mal ne le veult tourner.
Amours, ainsi fault vos dons acheter,
Et vous donnez souvant sans ordonnance
15 Assez doulour et petit de plaisance,
Tout a rebours etc.

Pour .j. court temps le geu est aggreable,
Mais trop par est encombreux a user,
Et, ja soit il a dames honnorable,
20 A leurs servans est trop grief a porter.
Tousdiz convient souffrir et endurer,
Sans nul certain languir en esperance
Et recevoir mainte male meschance,
Tout a rebours etc.

Rubric A Balade, *C* Autra [Balad]—1 *C* Pardiu amour, *AB* amours—2 Que grans vo ben faytes c. c., *A* f. bien c., *B* f. comparer—3 *A* Voilles, *C* Au l.—4 *B* Rire p., *C* Ri en—5 *ABC* on doit—8 *AC* au r.—*Stanzas 2 and 3 inverted in C*—9 *A* est la m., *B* cest lamer, *C* mare au d.—10 *C* Car elha veult—11 *C* Et ne fait on ch.—12 *C* Quelh ne vueilhe trestout a mal t., *BC* vueille—13 *C* Ainsi convient vous dous chier a.—14 *C* Et recevpoir souvent en pacienca—15 *C* Asses dautruy en p.—16 *AC* au r.—17 *C* Pour pou de temps le ge nest, *A* bref temps—18 *C* angoisseux, *A* a passer—19 *C* ja soit il aux, *A* aux d.—20 *B* amis—21 *A* Tousjours, *C* Car i lheurs faut mains trevalhs ndurer—23 *C* Et endurer—24 *AC* au r.

    Parallels in Chaucer's 'Complaint of Venus' (line nos in parentheses) for which variants in Granson's poems have possible significance:
2 That men ful *dere* abye thy nobil thing (26)
4 *Wepynge to laughe,* and singe in compleynyng (28)
5 And doun to caste *visage and lokyng* (29)
7 All MSS of Chaucer's poem read 'Pleye in slepyng' (31), which editors amend to 'Pleyne.' All Granson MSS support the emendation with 'Plaindre' here.
9 Jelousie be hanged be a cable (33)
14 Which ofte he yiveth withouten *ordynaunce* (38)
15 As *sorwe* ynogh, and litel of pleasaunce (39)
18 But ful encomberous is the *usyng* (42)
21 Thus be we ever in *drede and sufferyng* (45)

Balade

Amours, sachiez que pas ne le veulz dire
Pour moy getter hors des amoureux las,
Car a porté si long temps mon martire
Qu'a mon vivant ne le guerpiray pas.
5   Il me souffit d'avoir tant de soulas
Que vëoir puisse la belle gracieuse;
Combien qu'elle est envers moy dangereuse
De li servir ne seray jamais las.

Certes, Amours, quant bien a droit remire
10 Les hauls estas, les moiens, et les bas,
Vous m'avez fait de tous les liex eslire,
A mon advis, le meilleur en tous cas.
Or ayme, Cuer, si fort com tu porras,
Car ja n'avras paine si douloureuse
15 Pour ma dame qui ne me soit joieuse
De li servir etc.

Cuer, il te doit assez plus que souffire
D'avoir choisi si bien que choisi as.
Ne querir plus royaume n'empire,
20 Car si bonne jamais ne trouveras,
Ne si belle par mes yeulx ne verras.
C'est jeunesse sachant et savoureuse;
Ja soit elle de m'amour desdaigneuse
De li servir etc.

Rubric A Balade, *C* Autra [Balada]—1 *A* saches . . . vueil, *C* le vou—3 *C* Car ja . . . le mart., *AB*
jay—4 *BC* Que—6 *C* puisa ma dama g., *B* belle *missing*—7 *C* quell soit, *B* vers—8 *AB* lui—9 *C* Et
par ma foy q., *B* bien dr.—11 *A* les biens, *B* les bons—12 *C* Pour bien servir l.—13 *AB* cuer ainsi
que tu, *C* quant tu—14 *C* Que ja neras, *B* naras—15 *C* quelh ne—16 *AB* lui—18 *B* ce que—19 *A* ne
dois querir, *B* ne quiers, *C* Or ne quir, *ABC* ne empire—20 *C* Car james si b.—21 *C* Ne par tes
yeulx si belha ne—22 *C* Jaune riant s.—23 *C* Car de tous biens est la plus cureuse—24 *AB* lui
    Parallels in Chaucer's 'Complaint of Venus' (line nos in parentheses) for which variants in
Granson's poem have possible significance:
1 But certes, love, *I* sey not in such wise (49)
3 For *I* so longe have been in your service (51)
9 And certis, Love, when I me *wel avise* (57)
11 Chese the best that ever *on erthe wente* (60)
13 Now *love well*, herte, and lok thou *never stente* (61)
18–19 That Love *so high* a grace to the sente (66)
    To chese *the worthieste* in alle wise (67)

APPENDIX B

Exchange between Jean Campion and Jean de le Mote

There are two MS texts of the ballade exchange between Philippe de Vitry and Jean de le Mote. The better text is in Penn and provides the basis for our edition above (II C). The second text, which supplies some readings for the edition, is Paris, Bibl. Nat. fonds latin 3343, a miscellany of prose and poetry, mainly Latin. In this MS, the exchange appears as the third and fourth poems in a connected series of six French ballades. The first two poems are lovers' complaints by Jean de le Mote. In the first a man complains, and in the second a woman. In both ballades there is abundant, often-obscure reference to mythological (or pseudo-mythological) personages. The poems seem to substantiate the complaint of Philippe that Jean fills his poems of love with 'noms divers' (see Philippe's poem, ll. 22–23).

The fifth and sixth poems in the series, which follow Philippe's attack and Jean's response, are the poems edited in this Appendix. In the fifth a poet named Jean Campion, a cleric of Tournai and follower of Philippe, takes up his mentor's attack on the misuse of names by 'le Mote.' In his ballade Philippe simply identified the target as 'Jehan,' but Campion not only employs the surname but also makes an oblique reference to le Mote's long poem, *Le Parfait du Paon* (ll. 1–3). In his poem Campion assures le Mote that he agrees with the man of Vitry that the Muses have nothing to do with his poems, and he invokes the punishments of Virgil's hell on him for the wild names he uses. With his own train of proper names stretched out through the poem, and especially with the three-line refrain enumerating the Muses, Campion seems to be parodying and answering his adversary's style.

Campion here uses the ten-line decasyllabic stanza that le Mote employed in answering Philippe. In responding to Campion, Jean employs the nine-line stanza with octosyllabic lines of Philippe's original poem. Predictably, he questions Campion's qualifications for criticizing the poetry of others and his understanding of literary reference. At the same time, he places him in a different category from Philippe, whose strictures he claims to welcome. Go and apply yourself to instructing rustics, he advises Campion.

Both poetic exchanges are lively and obviously written with feeling, though at the same time the scholars' intellectual pretensions provide much of the matter and some of the fire. The second debate has a particular interest here, as the first one does, because it probably represents an exchange across the Channel. We can only guess that the contention ended with le Mote having the last word. Chaucer may well have known the whole series of six ballades.

While the following edition is made from the MS, it differs from that of Pognon (ref.

in n. 16 above) only in minor details, and some punctuation and capitalization. Pognon's introduction and notes provide a good deal of information about the poems and their many references, though he admits he does not understand all that is meant. I do not either. One may be confident that both purposeful obscurity and considerable corruption in the MS text contribute to the difficulty.

Messire Jehan Campions [f.110v]

[I] Sur Parnase a le Mote Cyrre et Nise,
Cuide avoir chilz songié, qui le Parfait
Des Vens imparfist, et beu a devise
De la fontene Elycone que a fait
Li chevaulx volans, dont moult s'a mesfait—
Che dist li Victriens, dieus d'armonie—
Car ne congnoist ne congneu. Mené
Ne l'i ont Clyo, Euterpe, Uranie,
Thersicore, Erato, Melponené,
Thalye, Calliope, et Polimnie.

Espoir! Caron en Phlegeton l'esprise,
Ou Athleto en Lethés l'out attrait,
Ou en Cochite ou Thesiphone est prise,
Pour lui mectre el point qu'elle Athamas lait,
Quant en ses dis noms de Bretesque mait
Que n'ont congneu poete en Meonie, [f.111r]
En Manthe, en Peligne, en Verone né,
Ne Flaccus, Clyo, Euterpe, Uranie, etc.

Si lo que se dis de le femme Anchise
Ou de son fil l'archier volage estrait,
Taise tez noms! Mieulx en vaulra s'emprise.
Et se l'avule en Ramnuse o son lait
L'a allechié, je les talaire n'ait
Persé, harpen; ne egyde Gorgonie
Syringe ou barbiton l'ait demené,
A l'onnour Clyo, Euterpe, Uranie,
Thersicore, Erato, Melpomené,
Thalye, Calliope, Polimnie.

Jehan de le Mote respond audit
Messire Jehan Campion

Tu, Campions, appel faisans
Par le voye regalien,
Mote n'est point chevaulx volans,
Ains vit en le rieule Eliien.
Tu comprens le Philistiien
Et il David en combatant,
Par quoy en fleuve Tantalus
Te baigneront en argüant
Tribles, Florons, et Cerberus.

Sces tu tous les mondains rommans
Et tous les noms, .V. et combien?
Je doubt que li fruis des lubans
Vraiement ne soient li tien.
Il ne m'en cault du Victrien;

76

Son castoy pren de cuer joyant.
Mais tu! Va, s'apren bergibus!
La tiennent escole de cant
Tribles, Florons etc.

Tu, qui tous vens yes congnoissans,
Congnois tu le Mur Graciien,
Le roc ou Phebus est regnans,
Et tous les clans de cel engien
Et de Cerberus le Mairien?
Nennil, certes. Mais d'Aridant
Congnistras au fons la jus,
Car la te menront galopant
Tribles, Florons, et Cerberus.

[f.111v]

PART III

The Contents of Penn

A. THE SIGNIFICANCE OF THE CONTENTS
OF THE MANUSCRIPT

For the student of literature University of Pennsylvania MS French 15 is by far the most interesting extant anthology of fourteenth century French lyrics. There exist from the time a number of important collections of the works of a single author: the Machaut manuscripts; the great Deschamps collection in the Bibliotheque Nationale, f.fr. 840; the two Froissart manuscripts, B.N., f.fr. 830 and 831. There are also major chansonniers which assemble the words and music of a variety of fine lyrics, such as the Codex Reïna (B.N., f.fr., n.a. 6771) and the collection that belongs to the Musée Condé; in these, however, the interest of the words is unavoidably secondary to that of the music. No manuscript collection of poetic texts by various authors has come down to us which rivals Penn in importance.[1] The quality of the selection is high, the range of the subjects and forms is wide, and the arrangement of the works reflects the thought and planning of a sensitive reader of literature, perhaps Oton de Granson or another friend of Chaucer. The contents of Penn provide a unique source of information about educated literary tastes and predilections in the fourteenth century, and they hold particular additional interest for Chaucerians.

Other than Giulio Bertoni's defective inventory of Penn,[2] there has been no published list of its contents. Charles Mudge's dissertation corrected Bertoni's errors,[3] but it has not been published. The list which follows here is indebted to Mudge's 'List of Incipits' for the check it provided on the numbering of the poems, on the transcription of the incipits, and on the record of manuscripts and editions. I have corrected and substantially supplemented Mudge's information on these items, and have presented in addition an analysis of the versification of each work as well as individual notes on many of the lyrics which cover matters such as the relationships of the poems to each other, the existence of musical notations for the pieces, points of special interest about the poems, and Chaucerian connections. Except in remarking musical notation that exists for certain of the poems, these notes are not systematic; they are instead meant to be suggestive.

Among numerous indications of the anthologist's care in arranging the contents of Penn are the customary alternation of forms, the maintenance of natural groups of works (for instance, double and triple ballades), the frequent matching of poems in which men are the speakers with poems in which women speak, the varying of topics and the treatments of them, and the groupings of the works of Machaut and Granson. In Penn the metrics generally conform to the *formes fixes* practice of the century. A word perhaps is needed about the entries for the rondeaux and virelays. Both forms begin (and end) with their refrains, so the incipit of each poem is the first line of the refrain. This I have entered as the 'incipit,' and for the 'refrain' I have used the second line of the refrain, adding 'etc.' if the refrain goes beyond two lines. With the virelays I have indicated the rhyme schemes up to the point that repetition begins.

Following are the salient physical features of Penn: It is of well-preserved parchment, its hundred folios measuring 30 by 24.2 cm. The poems are written in an attractive Gothic script throughout, probably by more than one scribe. The first folio begins with the rubric:

> Ci sensuient plusieurs bonnes
> pastourelles complaintes lays
> et Ballades et autres choses

Mudge, pp. 2–3, describes the concluding folios as follows: 'Lyric 310 ends on fol. 92d. On fol. 93a are five verses of a Petrarchan sonnet in a fifteenth-century Italian hand. Folios 93b to 95d are ruled, but blank. On fol. 96a is the beginning of an alphabetical index of incipits in a fifteenth-century Italian hand. The heading reads: "Rubricha infrascripta est per alphabetum." Folios 96b to 100b are ruled, but blank. At the top of fol. 100c in a third and different fifteenth-century Italian hand, are two verses of an Italian poem.'

B. KEY TO ABBREVIATIONS FOR MANUSCRIPTS

(The following list includes all MSS which contain more than one poem also found in Univ. of Pennsylvania MS French 15.)

Machaut Manuscripts: MSS wholly or primarily made up of works by Guillaume de Machaut.

A   Paris, Bibliothèque Nationale fonds français 1584—102 texts in Penn (contains musical settings)

B   Paris, B.N.f.fr. 1585—90 texts (musical settings)

C   Paris, B.N.f.fr. 1586—61 texts (musical settings)

D   Paris, B.N.f.fr. 1587—46 texts (words only)

E   Paris, B.N.f.fr. 9221—99 texts (musical settings)

F   Paris, B.N.f.fr. 22545—17 texts (musical settings)

G   Paris, B.N.f.fr. 22546—94 texts (musical settings)

H   Paris, B.N.f.fr. 881—16 texts (words only)

J   Paris, Bibl. de l'Arsenal 5203—20 texts (words only)

K   Bern, Burgerbibliothek 218—8 texts (words only)

M   Paris, B.N.f.fr. 843—94 texts (words only)

Pep   Cambridge, Magdalene Col., Pepysian Lib. 1594—3 texts (musical settings)

PM   New York, Pierpont Morgan Lib. M.396—18 texts (musical settings)

Vg   New York, Gallery Wildenstein—90 texts (formerly Voguë MS; musical settings)

Granson Manuscripts (Granson composed no music)

GrA   Neuchâtel, Bibliothèque Arthur Piaget, VIII—27 texts

GrB   Paris, B.N.f.fr. 2201—13 texts

GrC   Barcelona, Biblioteca Catalunya 8—8 texts

Other Manuscripts

Cam   Cambrai, Bibl. Communale 1328—3 texts (repertory MS with music)

Ch   Chantilly, Musée Condé 1047—5 texts (repertory MS with music)

DeA   Paris, B.N.f.fr. 840—1 text (the major Deschamps collection)

DeB   Paris, B.N.f.fr., n.a.6221—15 texts (words only; works mainly of Deschamps, but some anonymous and by Machaut)

Fl   Florence, Bibl. Nazionale Centrale, Panciatichi 26—2 texts (repertory MS with music)

Mo   Modena, Bibl. Estense, 5.24—2 texts (repertory MS with music)

PI   Paris, B.N.fonds italien 568—2 texts

Pg   Prague, Bibl. Univ., XI.E9—2 texts (repertory MS with music)

PR   Paris, B.N.f.fr., n.a. 6771—6 texts (repertory MS with music; Codex Reïna)

Str   Strasbourg, Bibl. de la Ville, m.222.c.22—4 texts (repertory MS with music; destroyed but index survives)

Tr   Chateau de Serrant (Maine-et-Loire), Bibl. de la Duchesse de la Tremoïlle—6 texts (table of contents only survives)

Ut   Utrecht, Universiteitsbibliotheek 6E37—2 texts (repertory MS with music)

Vit   Paris, B.N.fonds latin 3343—2 texts (contains exchange between Vitry and le Mote; no music)

We   Westminster Abbey Library 21—10 texts (words only)

Z   Paris, B.N.f.fr.1131—2 texts

C. KEY TO ABBREVIATIONS FOR EDITIONS

(The list includes all standard editions of the poems contained in Univ. of Pennsylvania MS French 15 and most other editions.)

1. Apel, Willi, ed. *French Secular Compositions of the Fourteenth Century*, with edition of the literary texts by Samuel N. Rosenberg. Corpus Mensurabilis Musicae, 53. 3 vols. American Institute of Musicology, 1970–72.
2. Bertoni, Giulio. 'Liriche di Oton de Grandson, Guillaume de Machaut e di altri poeti in un nuovo canzoniere.' *Archivum Romanicum*, 16 (1932), 1–20.
3. Chichmaref. Vladimir Fedorovich, ed, *Guillaume de Machaut: Poésies lyriques*. 2 vols. Paris: Champion, 1909.
4. Hoepffner, Ernest, ed. *Oeuvres de Guillaume de Machaut*. 3 vols. Société des anciens textes français. Paris: Firmin–Didot, 1908–21.
5. *Le Jardin de Plaisance et Fleur de Réthorique: Réproduction en Facsimile de l'Edition publiée par Antoine Vérard vers 1501.* 2 vols. Paris: Firmin–Didot, 1910–24.
6. Kibler, William W. and James I. Wimsatt, eds. 'The Development of the Pastourelle in the Fourteenth Century: An Edition of Fifteen Poems with an Analysis' (forthcoming).
7. Ludwig, Friedrich. *Guillaume de Machaut: Musikalische Werke*. 4 vols. Leipzig: Breitkopf, 1926–43.
8. Monod, Bernard. *Quinze poésies inédites de Guillaume de Machaut*. Versailles, 1903.
9. Mudge, Charles R. *The Pennsylvania Chansonnier: A Critical Edition of Ninety-five Anonymous Ballades from the Fourteenth Century*. Univ. of Indiana Diss. Ann Arbor: Univ. Microfilms, 1972.
10. Orsier, Joseph. *Un Ambassadeur de Savoie en Angleterre, poète d'amour, précurseur de Charles d'Orleans, Othon III de Grantson*. 2nd ed. Paris: Champion, 1921.
11. Pagès, Amadée, ed. *La Poésie française en Catalogne du XIIIᵉ siècle à la fin du XVᵉ siècle*. Bibliothèque Méridionale, Iʳᵉ Série, T. XXIII. Paris: Didier, 1936.
12. Paris, Paulin, ed. *Le Livre du Voir Dit de Guillaume de Machaut*. Paris: La Société des Bibliophiles François, 1875.
13. Piaget, Arthur. *Oton de Grandson, sa vie et ses poésies*. Mémoires et documents publiés par la Société d'Histoire de la Suisse Romande, 3ᵉ Serie, T. I. Lausanne: Payot, 1941.
14. Raynaud, Gaston and le marquis de Queux de Saint-Hilaire, eds. *Oeuvres complètes d'Eustache Deschamps*. Société des Anciens textes Français. 11 vols. Paris: Firmin–Didot, 1878–1903.
15. Schirer, G. Ludwig. *Oton de Granson und seine Dichtungen*. Strassburg: Du Mont–Schauberg, 1904.
16. Schrade, Leo, ed. *The Works of Guillaume de Machaut*. Vols. II–III, *Polyphonic Music of the Fourteenth Century*. Monaco: Editions du Lyre, 1956.
17. Tarbé, Prosper, ed. *Les Oeuvres de Guillaume de Machaut*. Paris, 1849.
18. ——, ed. *Poésies d'Agnès de Navarre–Champagne, Dame de Foix*. Paris, 1856. (Tarbé supposed that this lady wrote Machaut's lyrics in which a woman is the speaker.)
19. Henry A. Todd, ed. *Le Dit de la Panthère d'Amours*. Société des Anciens Textes Français. Paris: Firmin–Didot, 1883.
20. Pognon, E. 'Ballades mythologiques de Jean de le Mote, Philippe de Vitri, Jean Campion.' *Humanisme et Renaissance*, 5 (1938), 385–417.
21. Wilkins, Nigel E., ed. *A Fourteenth-Century Repertory from the Codex Reïna (Paris,*

Bibl. Nat., Nouv. Acq. Fr. 6771). Corpus Mensurabilis Musicae, XXXVI. American Institute of Musicology, 1966.

22. ——, ed. *La Louange des Dames by Guillaume de Machaut.* New York: Barnes & Noble, 1972.
23. ——, ed. *One Hundred Ballades, Rondeaux and Virelays from the Late Middle Ages.* London: Cambridge Univ. Press, 1969.
24. Wimsatt, James I. *Chaucer and the Poems of 'Ch.'* Cambridge: Brewer, 1982.

D. LIST OF CONTENTS OF UNIVERSITY OF PENNSYLVANIA MS FRENCH 15

1. f.1a   [Pastourelle]

    Inc: [U]n veil pastoure nomme hermans
    Refr: Je le weil aussi le veult dieux
    Metr: 5 sts. ababccddedE; envoy, ddeddE; octosyllabics.
    Eds: 2 6

The first fifteen poems of Penn make a coherent group of five-stanza works, twelve pastourelles and three serventois, composed in Picard dialect in early and mid fourteenth century. No doubt they were written for the bourgeois puys rather than for the courts, for which the remaining poems in Penn seem to have been composed. See II.E above.

2. f.1c   Pastourelle

    Inc: Robin seoit droit delez un perier
    Refr: Par la vertu de constellacion
    Metr: 5 sts. ababbccddeddE; envoy, ddeddE; decasyllabics.
    Ed: 6

3. f.2a   Pastourelle

    Inc: En un friche vers un marchais
    Refr: Se je truis mon proufit a faire
    Metr: ababbccdcD; no envoy; octosyllabics.
    Ed: 6

4. f.2b   Pastourelle

    Inc: Desa amiens plusieurs bergiers trouvay
    Refr: Comment uns homs puet estre si quetis
          Envers uns autres ne si infortunez.
    Metr: 5 sts. ababccddeDE; envoy, ddeDE; decasyllabics.
    Ed: 6

5. f.2d   Pastourelle de Justice

    Inc: Plusieurs bergiers et bergerelles
    Refr: Justice en va en ynde pour manoir (first half variable)
    Metr: 5 sts. ababbccdcD; envoy, ccdcD; decasyllabics.
    Ed: 6

6. f.3b   Pastourelle

    Inc: Trois bergiers dancien aez
    Refr: Un leu pour garder les oeilles
    Metr: 5 sts. ababbccddeeffgG; envoy, ffgG; octosyllabics.
    Ed: 6

The metrics of this poem and the next have a significant likeness to Froissart's pastourelles. In addition, both poems have historical and geographical references which suggest composition in or near Froissart's (and England's Queen Philippa's) homeland about 1360 or shortly before.

7. f.3d   Pastourelle

Inc: Madoulz li bergiers et ses fieulx
Refr: Aussi tost com crie St george
Metr: 5 sts. ababbccddeeffgfG; envoy, ffgfG; octosyllabics.

This pastourelle concerns the bands of pillagers who roamed northern France in the 1350's and 1360's, crying 'St George.' But the cry did not mean they were English; in this case, they were Boulenois.

8. f.4c   Pastourelle amoureuse

Inc: Robin seoit et maret a plains camps
Refr: Par le corps dieu et vous ferez que sage (first half variable)
Metr: 5 sts. ababbccbbddbD; envoy, bbdD; decasyllabics.
Ed: 6

9. f.5a   Pastourelle

Inc: En un marchais de grant antiquite
Refr: Argus perdi sa femme vrayement
      Quot nom yo et si avoit c. yeulx
Metr: 5 sts. ababccdCD; envoy, ccdCD; decasyllabics.
Ed: 6

10. f.5c   Pastourelle

Inc: Onques ne fu en mon dormant songans
Refr: Depuis le temps nabugodonozor (first half-line variable)
Metr: 5 sts. ababbccdcD; envoy, ccdcD; decasyllabics.
Ed: 6

This 'pastourelle,' and poems 11 and 15, which are called 'serventois,' are dream visions, though dream visions are typical of neither genre. This dream is under the aegis of the fairies.

11. f.5d   Serventois amoureux

Inc: En avisant les esches atalus
Refr: Quonques ne fist orpheus ne seraine
Metr: 5 sts. ababbccdcD; envoy, cdcD; decasyllabics.
Ed: 6

In this dream vision the narrator sees marvels assisted by the guidance of the 'eagle of Theseus' and the 'horse of Jason.' Certain matters of structure and content suggest Chaucer's *House of Fame*; e.g., when the narrator looks out of the eagle's beak, he sees beasts of the zodiac; and the second of the two places he visits is the 'ostel Dedalus.'

12. f.6b   Pastourelle amoureuse

Inc: Es plus lons jours de la Saint Jehan deste
Refr: Corps gracieux vrays humains paradis
Metr: 3 sts. ababbccbbdbD; envoy, bbdbD; decasyllabics.
Ed: 6

The bergère in this poem inverts the *aubade* convention by reproaching the sun and the day for leaving too soon. One is reminded of Chaucer's resuscitation of the aubade in *Troilus* and the Reeve's Tale.

13. f.6d   Serventois pastourel

> Inc: Samours nestoit plus puissant que nature
> Metr: 5 sts. ababccddc; ddc; decasyllabics.
> Ed: 6

Indications of early date for this poem include its lack of a refrain, and its sharing stanza openings with a poem of Brisebarre le Court, who died before 1340. Our serventois may have been written for the same poetic contest as Brisebarre's. See Mudge, pp. 247–48.

14. f.7a   Pastourelle

> Inc. Decha brimeu sur un ridel
> Refr: Tant grate chievre que gist mal
> Metr: 5 sts. aabaabbccdccD; envoy, ccD; octosyllabics except short 6th lines.
> Ed: 6

15. f.7c   Serventois

> Inc: Par bas cavech et pesant couverture
> Refr: Qui se nommoit fortune la dervee (first half-line variable)
> Metr: ababbccdcD; envoy, ccdecD; decasyllabics.
> Ed: 6

This dream vision is a political allegory, utilizing heraldic symbols, which involves the leopard of England (Edward III), the black lion of Flanders (prob. Louis de Male), and the fleur de lis of France. Fortune taunts the leopard that his luck is gone.

16. f.8a   Balade

> Inc: La char dor fin gemme mena phebus
> Refr: Cicropiens le clergie de bachus
> Metr: 3 sts. ababbabA; decasyllabics.
> Ed: 9

Mudge, p. 150, includes this among 'corrupt' and 'insoluble' works in Penn. Its heavy use of often-obscure classical reference resembles that for which Vitry and Campion criticized Jean de le Mote.

17. f.8b   Balade

> Inc: Qui est de moy vivant plus dolereux
> Refr: Pointe trenchant regart de basilique
> Metr: 3 sts. ababbcbC; decasyllabics.
> Ed: 9

18. f.8c   Complaint de pastour et de pastourelle amoureuse

> Inc: Une jeune gentil bergiere
> Auth: Oton de Granson
> Metr: 19 sts ababbccdeD; decasyllabics.

MSS: GrA GrB GrC; Paris, BN f.fr.1131; f.fr.24440; Carpentras, Bibl. Inguimbertine, fr.390.
Eds: 10 11 13 15 17

19. f.10a   Balade

Inc: Pitagoras en ses chancons divines
Refr: Fors seulement que de trompe et de harpe
Metr: 3 sts. ababccddedE; decasyllabics.
Ed: 9

Music is the subject of this ballade, but it evidently was not set to music. With the reference to Pythagoras, one might compare Chaucer's *Book of the Duchess*, l. 1167. The texts abound with such allusions.

20. f.10b   Balade

Inc: Salus assez par bonne entencion
Refr: Car le couroux ny vault pas une maille
Auth: Oton de Granson
Metr: 3 sts. ababbccdcD; envoy, ccdcD; decasyllabics.
MSS: GrA GrB GrC; Paris, Bibl. Rothschild 2796.
Eds: 10 11 13 15

Only twelve ballades in Penn have envoys, and this is the only one before No. 229. Envoys came to be added to ballades in the latter part of the fourteenth century.

21. f.10c   Balade

Inc: Je congnois bien les tourmens amoureux
Refr: Qui fondre peust et lui renouveller (first half-line variable)
Auth: Oton de Granson
Metr: 3 sts. ababbccddedE; decasyllabics.
MS: GrA   Ed: 13

22. f.10d   Balade

Inc: Je vous choisy noble loyal amour
Refr: Que nulle autre jamais ne choisiray
Auth: Oton de Granson
Metr: 3 sts. ababbcbC; decasyllabics.
MSS: GrA GrB; Brussels, Bibl. Royale 10961–70
Eds: 5 13 15

Except for the refrain and line 23, all lines begin 'Je vous choisy.' The poem is called 'Balade de Saint Valentin' in MS Gr2, and an Envoy is added to it in Ed 5.

23. f.11a   Balade

Inc: Jay en mon cuer j. oeil qui toudiz veille
Refr: Qui mon cuer voit toudiz ou que je soye
Auth: Oton de Granson
Metr: 3 sts. ababbccdcD; decasyllabics.
MS: GrA   Ed: 2 13

24. f.11b   Balade

Inc: Loyal amour ardant et desireuse

86

Auth: Oton de Granson
Refr: Que de riens plus ne me souvient par mame
     Fors que amour et de ma belle dame
Metr: 3 sts. ababbccDD; decasyllabics.
MS: GrA   Ed: 13

25. f.11c   La complainte de lan nouvel

Inc: Jadis mavint que par merancolie
Auth: Oton de Granson
Metr: 8 sts. ababbcbc; decasyllabics.
MSS: GrA GrB GrC   Eds: 10 11 13 15

In MS GrB the title is 'La complainte de lan nouvel que Gransson fist pour un chevalier quil escoutoit complaindre.' Its situation imitates that of the dream in Chaucer's *Book of the Duchess.*

26. f.12a   Complainte

Inc: Je souloye de mes yeulx avoir joye
Auth: Oton de Granson
Metr: 12 sts. aaabaaabbbbabbba; decasyllabic except every fourth line tetrasyllabic.
MSS: GrA GrB   Eds: 13 15

The first letters of the first six stanzas form the name ISABEL. Cf. poem No. 27. The reference is probably to Isabel of York in the first place, and perhaps to Isabel of Bavaria in the second. See note 2 to II above.

27. f.13b   Souhait en complainte

Inc: Il me convient par souhait conforter
Auth: Oton de Granson
Metr: 64 ll. decasyllabic couplets
MSS: GrA GrB   Ed: 13 15

The rubric originally in the MS was 'Le Souhait Saint Valentin' (as in GrB), but was altered. The first letters of the first six lines form the acrostic ISABEL; cf. No. 26. This and no. 106 are the only works in Penn in decasyllabic couplets.

28. 13d   Lestraine du jour de lan

Inc: Joye sante paix et honnour
Auth: Oton de Granson
Metr: 42 ll. octosyllabic couplets
MSS: GrA GrB   Eds: 10 13 15

29. f.14a   Le Lay de desir en complainte

Inc: Belle tournez vers moy vos yeulx
Auth: Oton de Granson
Metr: Lay form with 24 sts. in pairs, each with differing metrics, totalling 210 ll.
MS: GrA GrB   Eds: 10 13 15

A 165 ll. poem by Granson in BN f.fr.1131, edited separately in 13 and 15, opens with the same 21 ll. as this poem.

30. f.15c   Balade ('Complainte' effaced and 'Balade' superimposed)

Inc: Il nest confort qui tant de bien me face
Refr: Car chascun a joie de li loer
Auth: Oton de Granson
Metr: 3 sts. ababbccB; decasyllabics.
MSS: GrA GrB GrC
Eds: 11 13 15 24 (II Appendix A above)

This is the first of the series of five balades identified in MS GrB as 'Les Cinq Balades Ensievans.' Chaucer imitated the first, fourth, and fifth (our Nos 30, 33, and 34) in his 'Complaint to Venus.'

31. f.15d   Balade

Inc: A mon advis dieu raison et nature
Refr: Car trop par est son cuer plain de reffus
Auth: Oton de Granson
Metr: 3 sts. ababbccB; decasyllabics.
MSS: GrA GrB GrC   Eds: 11 13 15 24

The second of the Cinq Balades.

32. f.16a   Balade

Inc: Or est ainsi que pour la bonne et belle
Refr: Priez pour moy tous les loyaulx amans
Auth: Oton de Granson
Metr: 3 sts. ababbccB; decasyllabics.
MSS: GrA GrB GrC   Eds: 11 13 15 24

The third of the Cinq Balades.

33. f.16b   Balade

Inc: Certes amour cest chose convenable
Refr: Tout a rebours de ce quon veult trouver
Auth: Oton de Granson
Metr: 3 Sts. ababbccB; decasyllabics.
MSS: GrA GrB GrC   Eds: 11 13 15 24

The fourth of the Cinq Balades.

34. f.16c   Balade

Inc: Amours sachiez que pas ne le veulz dire
Refr: De li servir ne seray jamais las
Auth: Oton de Granson
Metr: 3 sts. ababbccB; decasyllabics.
MSS: GrA GrB GrC   Eds: 10 11 13 15 24

The fifth of the Cinq Balades.

35. f.16c   Balade

Inc: Dur moises de langoreuse mort
Refr: Vielle me lais qui jeune mas hussee
         Pour un annel de la fleur de soucie
Metr: 3 sts. ababbcBC; decasyllabics.
Ed: 9, 24 (Appendix I above)

As with No. 7, Mudge includes this with 'corrupt' and 'insoluble' texts. It is closely related to 'Ch' V (Penn No. 61).

36. f.16d   Balade

      Inc: Ce quay pense voulez que je vous die
      Refr: Il nest deduit qui vaille celui la
      Auth: Attributed to Guillaume de Machaut
      Metr: 3 sts. ababbcC; decasyllabics.
      MS: J   Ed: 3

Though it is found in the 'secondary' Machaut collection, MS J, the poem is probably not Machaut's.

37. f.17a   Balade

      Inc: Un vert jardin joly
      Refr: Fu ce bien songie
      Auth: Attributed to Guillaume de Machaut
      Metr: 3 sts. $a_7b_5a_7b_5b_5c_6b_5c_6$
      MS: J   Ed: 3

Ballades with short lines like this one are very rare in Penn. As with No. 36, it is probably not Machaut's. It tells the narrator's amorous dream.

38. f.17b   Balade

      Inc: Dedens mon cuer est pourtraite une ymage
      Refr: Resjois est quiconques la regarde
      Auth: Grimace
      Metr: 3 sts. ababbcC; decasyllabics.
      Ed: 1 9
      MS: Bern, Burgerbibliothek, A421

Bern MS presents first stanza only, with music. For Grimace, see II G above; cf. Nos 190, 191 below.

39. f.17b   Balade

      Inc: Onques mais namay/ne ne demenay
      Refr: Et point ne men refraindray
      Metr: 3 sts, $a_5a_5b_7a_5a_5b_7b_7a_7A_7$
      Ed: 9

Another ballade with short lines.

40. f.17c   Balade

      Inc: Esgare sui en divers destour
      Refr: Si vous suppli que madreciez en voye
      Metr: 3 sts. ababbcC; decasyllabics.
      Ed: 9

41. f.17d   Balade

      Inc: De bon eur en grant maleurete
      Refr: Je sui banis de bonne compaignie
      Metr: 3 sts. ababccdD; decasyllabics.
      MS: We   Ed: 9

42. f.18a   Balade

> Inc: Se tu monde estre veuls en ce monde
> Refr: Ou estre pues devoure dun seul louf (variable)
>   Quadroit nomme est cire mire bouf
> Metr: 3 sts. ababbbCC
> Ed: 9 24 (I Appendix)

Mudge includes the poem, p. 152, among the corrupt and insoluble. Its humor, however, is hardly inaccessible.

43. f.18b   [Balade]

> Inc: He loyaute bien te pues reposer
> Refr: Si est pitie quainsi loyaute dort
> Auth: Ascribed to Eustache Deschamps
> Metr: 3 sts. ababbcC; decasyllabics.
> MS: DeB   Ed: 14

Probably by Deschamps. See II D above.

44. f.18b   Balade

> Inc: Vous qui avez pour passer vostre vie
> Refr: Viellesce vient guerredon faut temps se passe
> Auth: Eustache Deschamps
> Metr: 3 sts. ababbcC; decasyllabics.
> MS: DeA DeB   Ed: 14

The only poem in Penn which appears in the major Deschamps collection, DeA. Deschamps quotes the first stanza in his *Art de Dictier* (Ed. 14, VII, 275).

45. f.18c   Balade

> Inc: Pymalion paris genevre helaine
> Refr: Prouver le puis pour vray comme evangile
>   Par salemon aristote et virgille
> Metr: 3 sts. ababccDD; decasyllabics.
> Ed: 9

This balade gives eleven examples of victims of Venus.

46. f.18d   Lay

> Inc: Sans avoir joye deport
> Metr: Does not adhere strictly to lay form. 24 sts., mostly paired,
>   mostly $a_7a_7a_7b_4a_7a_7a_7b_4$; 190 ll.

47. f.20b   Balade

> Inc: Quant plus regart le gracieux viaire
> Refr: Vivre sans lui bonnement ne porroye
> Metr: 3 sts. ababbcC; decasyllabics.
> Ed: 9

This is the first of a series of seven anonymous rhyme royal ballades, Machaut's favorite ballade form. A devoted lover is the speaker in all seven.

48. f.20c   Balade

Inc: Dame qui jain plus quautre creature
Refr: Comment vous ain de cuer de corps et darme
Metr: 3 sts. ababbcC; decasyllabics.
Ed: 9

49. f.20d   Balade

Inc: Il a longtemps quen moy maint j. desir
Refr: Affin que soit de mamour plus certaine
Metr: 3 sts. ababbcC; decasyllabics.
Ed: 9

50. f.20d   Balade

Inc: Amours me fist recevoir grant honnour
Refr: De la belle qui mes mauls tient en cure
Metr: 3 sts. ababbcC; decasyllabics.
Ed: 9

51. f.21a   Balade

Inc: La grant doucour et le courtois parler
Refr: Si doulcement quil nest riens qui manoye
Metr: 3 sts. ababbcC; decasyllabics.
Ed: 9

52. f.21b   Balade

Inc: Ne scay comment .j. cuer plain de doulour
Refr: Se longuement my faloit demourer
Metr: 3 sts. ababbcC; decasyllabics.
Ed. 9

53. f.20d   Balade

Inc: Helas bien voy quil me couvient finer
Refr: Et a ma dame aussi me recommans
Metr: 3 sts. ababbcC; decasyllabics.
Ed: 9

This is a rhyme royal lover's testament, comparable to Criseyde's in *Troilus* IV
771–91, and Troilus', V 295–315.

54. f.21c   Balade

Inc: Je ne puis trop amour louer
Refr: Et quanque jay desbatement
Metr: 3 sts. ababcdcD; octosyllabics.
Ed: 9

55. f.21d   Balade

Inc: Se veuls aujourdhui vivre en paix
Refr: Cest la chose dont plus tennorte

Auth: Attributed to Eustache Deschamps
Metr: 3 sts. ababcdcD; decasyllabics.
MSS: DeB; BN f.fr. 1140, 5727, 25434, n.a. 10032; Berlin, Kupfer-stichkabinett, 78 B 17; Cambrai, Bibl. Mun. 811–12; Epinal, Bibl. de la Ville, 189; Rome, Vatican Ottobuona 1212; Turin, L.IV.3.
Eds: 5 14

Considering that it is an anonymous text without music, this ballade is contained in an extraordinary number and range of MSS. It has the popular moral tone of much of Deschamps' poetry, and is probably his.

56. f.22a   Balade

Inc: Ou estes vous joye et esbatement
Refr: Donc en doulour me faut user ma vie
Metr: 3 sts. ababbcC; decasyllabics.
Ed: 9

57. f.22b   Balade

Inc: De toutes roses ne qui qun seul bouton
Refr: Qui comparee puet estre a absalon
Metr: 3 sts. ababbcbC; decasyllabics.
Ed: 9

58. f.22b   Balade

Inc: Harpe rote eschiquier ciphonie
Refr: Me het de mort cest ma dame mamie
Metr: 3 sts. ababbcbC; decasyllabics.
Ed: 9

59. f.22c   Balade

Inc: Je croy quil nest creature mondaine
Refr: Nest que tristour dont mon las cuer lermoye
Metr: 3 sts. ababbcC; decasyllabics.
Ed: 9

60. f.22d   Balade

Inc: A vous dame humblement me complains
Refr: Vray cuer gentilz pour vostre amour morray
Metr: 3 sts. ababccdD; decasyllabics.
Ed. 9

61. f.23a   Balade

Inc: Se la puissant royne semiramis
Refr: Tant que je peusse ma dame en aide avoir
Metr: 3 sts. ababccddeefF; decasyllabics.
Ed: 9

This poem provides probably the earliest extant list of the Neuf Preuses (Female Worthies), which Deschamps has been supposed to originate (See Ed. No. 14, XI, 226–27; and Ann McMillan, *Mediævalia* 5 [1979], 137, n. 11). In the light of the multiple classical allusions, and the poem's position in Penn immediately preceding the exchange between Philippe de Vitry and Jean de le Mote, we might suppose the author to be Jean. The Neuf Preux were originated by Jacques de Longuyon in his Alexander romance, *Les Voeux du paon* (c.1310). Jean, whose *Parfait du Paon* is a continuation of Jacques' poem, would be a likely originator of the Preuses.

62. f.23b   Balade

Inc: De terre en grec gaule appellee
Refr: En albion de dieu maldicte
Auth: Philippe de Vitry
Metr: 3 sts. ababbcdcD; octosyllabic except fifth lines have 4 syllables.
MS: Vit   Eds: 9 20 24 (II C above)

Mudge relegates this and the following poem by Jean de le Mote to his 'obscure' classification. Pognon (Ed. No. 20) edits only MS Vit.

63. f.23c   La Response

Inc: O victriens mondains dieu darmonie
Refr: De terre en grec gaulle de dieu amee
Auth: Jean de le Mote
Metr: 3 sts. ababbccdcD; decasyllabics.
MS: Vit   Eds: 9 20 24 (II C above)

For poems which provide a sequel to this exchange, found in MS Vit, see II Appendix B.

64. f.23d   Lay

Inc: Se fortune destinee et menee
Metr: 150 ll. of from four to ten syllables divided into sixteen sts. of varying length, not usually paired. It has the length, but not the set form prescribed for the lay.

65. f.25a   Balade

Inc: Amour vraye en paix seurement
Refr: Dont fait il bon vivre amoureusement
Metr: 3 sts. ababbcbC; decasyllabics.
Ed: 9

66. f.25f   Balade

Inc: Bien appartient a dame de hault pris
Refr: A dieu comment douceur et sa beaute
Metr: 3 sts. ababbcC; decasyllabics.
Ed: 9

67. f.25b   Balade

Inc: Raison se seigne et honneur se merveille
Refr: Mon cuer mamour mesperance ma joye
Metr: 3 sts. ababbcC; decasyllabics.
Ed: 9

68. f.25c   Balade

Inc: Bien doy amours parfaitement loer
Refr: Sen loe amours et vous madame aussi
Metr: 3 sts. ababbcC; decasyllabics.
Ed: 9

69. f.25d   Balade

Inc: Maint amant ay veu desconforter
Refr: Dont sens raison font plaintes et clamours
Auth: Attributed to Eustache Deschamps
Metr: 3 sts. ababccdD; decasyllabics.
MS: DeB   Ed: 14

Probably not by Deschamps. See II D above.

70. f.26a   Balade

Inc: Se cruaulte felonnie et regour
Refr: Saroient il ce croy pitie de mi
Metr: 3 sts. ababbcC; decasyllabics.
Ed: 9

71. f.26a   Balade

Inc: Se dieu me doint de vostre amour jouir
Refr: Honneur deduit bien paix sante ne joye
Metr: 3 sts. ababbcC; decasyllabics.
Ed: 9

Mudge, p. 264, notes that the incipit is like that of a Machaut ballade, 'Se Dieux me
doint de ma dame joir.' The similarity extends no further.

72. f.26b   Balade

Inc: Qui des couleurs sauroit a droit jugier
Refr: Que fin azur loyaute segnefie
Auth: Guillaume de Machant
Metr: 3 sts. ababccdD; decasyllabics.
MS: G   Ed: 3 22 23

Since this ballade appears only in the latest 'primary' Machaut collection, it was
probably composed after 1364 and is the latest of the poems of Machaut in Penn.
The color symbolism suggests Chaucer's *Anelida and Arcite*, ll. 145–46, 180, 330,
and the refrain of 'Against Women Unconstant.'

73. f.26c   Balade

Inc: Certes mes plours ne font que commancier
Refr: Amour le veult et mon cuer si ottrie
Metr: 3 sts. ababbcC; decasyllabics.
Ed: 9

74. f.26d   Balade

Inc: Il a long temps quamay premierement
Refr: Mais quant li plaist en gre recoy la mort

Metr: 3 sts. ababbcC; decasyllabics.
MS: We   Ed: 9

75. f.26d   Balade

Inc: Trop me merveil de ce monde present
Refr: Car ilz ne sont remery de personne
Metr: 3 sts. ababcdcD; decasyllabics.
Ed: 9

76. f.27a   Balade

Inc: Toutes vertus voy au jour dui perir
Refr: Dont nuit et jour mon cuer sueffre martire
Metr: 3 sts. ababbcbC; decasyllabics.

77. f.27b   Balade

Inc: A justement considerer
Refr: On na que sa vie en ce monde
Auth: Attributed to Eustache Deschamps
Metr: ababbcC; seven-syllable lines.
MS: DeB   Ed: 14

Probably by Deschamps.

78. f.27c   Lay

Inc: Se pour doulereux tourment
Metr: Approx. lay form; 24 sts., generally paired, each pair with
differing metrics; 191 ll.

79. f.29a   Balade

Inc: Se la sage rebeque estoit vivant
Refr: Par fausse envie et langue envenimee
Metr: 3 sts. ababccdD; decasyllabics except seven-syllable fifth lines.
Ed: 9

80. f.29b   Balade

Inc: Aspre reffus contre doulce priere
Refr: Pour bien servir ay je tel guerredon
Metr: 3 sts. ababbcC; decasyllabics.
Eds: 5 9

81. f.29b   Rondel

Inc: Doulce dame quant vers vous fausseray
Refr: Tout bien deveroit en mon cuer defaillir
Auth: Guillaume de Machaut
Metr: 8 ll. ABaAabAB; decasyllabics.
MSS: A B C D E G H M Vg
Eds: 3 17 22

Nos 81–120 are all by Machaut; Nos 81–113 all appear in MSS in Machaut's
Louange des dames (lyrics not set to music).

95

82. f.29c   Balade

        Inc: Dame plaisant nette et pure
        Refr: Sainsi nest que ne vous voye
        Auth: Guillaume de Machaut
        Metr: 6 sts. ababbcC; seven-syllable lines.
        MSS: A B C D E G H J K M Vg
        Eds: 3 22 23

In other MSS the rubric is 'Balade double.'

83. f.29d   Rondel

        Inc: Mon cuer qui mis en vous son desir a
        Refr: Mourra sa lui ne vous voit desiree
        Auth: Guillaume de Machaut
        Metr: 8 il. ABaAabAB; decasyllabics.
        MSS: A B C D E H M Vg
        Eds: 3 22

84. f.29d   Balade

        Inc: Il nest doulour desconfort ne tristece
        Refr: Et tout pour vous beaulz doulz loyaulz amis
        Auth: Guillaume de Machaut
        Metr: 3 sts. ababccdD; decasyllabics.
        MSS: A B C D E J M Vg
        Eds: 3 12 18 22

Besides *Louange* this poem appears in *Voir Dit.*

85. f.30a   Rondel

        Inc: Cuer corps desir povoir vie et usage
        Refr: En vous servir doulce dame mis ay
        Auth: Guillaume de Machaut
        Metr: 8 ll. ABaAabAB; decasyllabics.
        MSS: A B C D E G M Vg   Eds: 3 22

86. f.30a   Balade

        Inc: Trop est crueulz le mal de jalousie
        Refr: Il vaurroit mieux cent contre un estre coux
        Auth: Guillaume de Machaut
        Metr: 3 sts. ababbcC; decasyllabics.
        MSS: A B D E G H M Vg   Eds: 3 17 22

The sentiment that it is better to be a cuckold than jealous, would appeal to the Wife of Bath, though the narrator here—who is jealous—is prejudiced, as she is for a different reason.

87. f.30b   Rondel

        Inc: Blanche com lis plus que rose vermeille
        Refr: Resplendissant com rubis doriant
        Auth: Guillaume de Machaut
        Metr: 8 ll. ABaAabAB; decasyllabics.
        MSS: A B C D E G M Vg   Eds: 3 17 22

88. f.30c   Balade

Inc: Doulce dame vo maniere jolie
Refr: Durement vif et humblement lendure
Auth: Guillaume de Machaut
Metr: 3 sts. ababbcC; decasyllabics.
MSS: A B C D E G H M Vg DeB   Eds: 3 14 22

89. f.30c   Rondel

Inc: Dame je muir pous vous com pris
Refr: Pour bien amer dont mieux menprise
Auth: Guillaume de Machaut
Metr: ABaAbAB; decasyllabics.
MSS: A B C D E G M Vg   Eds: 3 22

90. f.30d   Balade

Inc: Nulz homs ne puet en amours prouffiter
Refr: Telle est damours la noble seignourie
Auth: Guillaume de Machaut
Metr: 3 sts. ababbcC; decasyllabics.
MSS: A B C D E G J K M Vg   Eds: 3 22

91. f.30d   Rondel

Inc: Partuez moy a louvrir de voz yeulx
Refr: Dame de qui mercy ne puis atraire
Auth: Guillaume de Machaut
Metr: 8 ll. ABaAabAB; decasyllabics.
MSS: A B C D E G H M Vg   Eds: 3 22

92. f.31a   Balade

Inc. Je ne sui pas de tel valour
Refr: Jay bien vaillant un cuer dami
Auth: Guillaume de Machaut
Metr: 3 sts. ababcdcD; octosyllabics.
MSS: A B C D E G H J K M Vg GrA   Eds: 3 13 18 22

93. f.31a   Chancon Royal

Inc: Onques mais nul nama si folement
Auth: Guillaume de Machaut
Metr: 5 sts. ababbccdd; envoy, dccd; decasyllabics.
MSS: A B C D E G H M Vg   Eds: 3 22 23

Six of the eight chants royaux that Machaut wrote are found among No. 93 to No.
104.

94. f.31c   Rondel

Inc: Par souhaidier est mes corps avec vous
Refr: Dame et mes cuers en tout temps y demeure
Auth: Guillaume de Machaut
Metr: 8 ll. ABaAabAB; decasyllabics.
MSS: A B C D E G H M Vg   Eds: 3 22

97

95. f.31d   Rondel

Inc: Trop est mauvais mes cuers quen .ij. ne part
Refr. Pour vous que jaim loyaument sans partie
Auth: Guillaume de Machaut
Metr: 8 ll. ABaAabAB; decasyllabics.
MSS: A B C D E G H M Vg   Eds: 3 22

96. f.31d   Chancon royal

Inc: Amour me fait desirer loyaument
Auth: Guillaume de Machaut
Metr: 5 sts. ababccddeed; envoy, deed; decasyllabics.
MSS: A B C D E G H J M Vg   Eds: 3 22

97. f.32b   Rondel

Inc: San cuer dolans de vous departiray
Refr: Et sans avoir joye jusques au retour
Auth: Guillaume de Machaut
Metr: 8 ll. ABaAabAB; decasyllabics:
MSS: A B C D E G H M Vg   Eds: 3 7 12 16 17 22

Besides in *Louange* this rondeau appears in the *Voir Dit* and set to music.

98. f.32b   Chancon Royal

Inc: Cuers ou mercy faut et cruautez y dure
Auth: Guillaume de Machaut
Metr: 5 sts. ababbccb; envoy, cbbc; decasyllabics.
MSS: A B C D E G H J M Vg   Eds: 3 22

99. f.32d   Rondel

Inc: Quant ma dame ne ma recongneu
Refr: Je doy moult bien sens perdre et congnoissance
Auth: Guillaume de Machaut
Metr: 8 ll. ABaAabAB; decasyllabics.
MSS: A B C D E G M Vg   Eds: 3 22

100. f.32d   Chancon royal

Inc: Je croy que nulz fors moy na tel nature
Auth: Guillaume de Machaut
Metr: 5 sts. ababccdd; envoy, dccd; decasyllabics.
MSS: A B C D E G H M Vg   Eds: 3 22

101. 33b   Rondel

Inc: De plus en plus ma grief doulour empire
Refr: Dont moult souvent mes cuers souspire et pleure
Auth: Guillaume de Machaut
Metr: 8 ll. ABaAabAB; decasyllabics.
MSS: A B C D E G M Vg   Eds: 3 22

102. 33b   Chancon royal

Inc: Se trestuit cil qui sont et ont este
Auth: Guillaume de Machaut
Metr: 5 sts. ababccddee; envoy, cddee; decasyllabics.
MSS: A B C D E G M Vg   Eds: 3 22

103. f.33d   Rondel

Inc: Pour dieu frans cuers soiez mes advocas
Refr: Vers mesdisans qui de mon bien nont cure
Auth: Guillaume de Machaut
Metr: 8 ll. ABaAabAB; decasyllabics.
MSS: A B C D E G M Vg   Eds: 3 22

104. f.33d   Chancon royal

Inc: Se loyautez et vertus ne puissance
Auth: Guillaume de Machaut
Metr: 5 sts. ababbccdd; envoy, ababbccdd; decasyllabics.
MSS: A B C D E G H M Vg   Eds: 3 22

105. f.34b   Rondel

Inc: Certes mon oeil richement visa bel
Refr: Quant premier vi ma dame bonne et belle
Auth: Guillaume de Machaut
Metr: ABaAabAB; decasyllabics.
MSS: A B D E G M Vg DeB   Eds: 3 5 7 16 22

Besides in *Louange* this rondel appears set to music; Deschamps quotes it in the *Art de Dictier* (Ed. No. 14, VII, 287).

106. f.34b   Balade [for Complainte]

Inc: Deux choses sont qui me font a martire
Auth: Guillaume de Machaut
Metr: 36 ll. decasyllabic couplets
MSS: A B D E G M Vg   Eds: 3 12 18

107. f.34c   Rondel

Inc: Doulce dame tant com vivray
Refr: Sera mes cuers a vos devis
Auth: Guillaume de Machaut
Metr: 8 ll. ABaAabAB; octosyllabics.
MSS: A B D E M Vg; Stockholm, Kungliga Biblioteket, Vu22.
Eds: 3 17 22

108. f.34d   Balade

Inc: Je prens congie aus dames a amours
Refr: Quant jay perdu la rien que plus amoye
Metr: 3 sts. ababccdD; decasyllabics.
Auth: Guillaume de Machaut
MSS: A E G M   Eds: 3 22

Troilus and Criseyde, I 543 and III 115, has imagery of tears similar to that in this ballade. Other echoes are found in Chaucer's 'Complaint to Pity' and 'Lak of Stedfastnesse.'

109. f.34d   Rondel

> Inc: Se tenir veulz le droit chemin donneur
> Refr: Ce que tu as aux bons liement donne
>   Et ce que n'as promet a chiere bonne
> Auth: Guillaume de Machaut
> Metr: 11 ll. ABBaAabbABB; decasyllabics.
> MSS: A B D E G M Vg   Eds: 3 22

110. f.35a   Complainte

> Inc: Amours tu mas tant este dure
> Auth: Guillaume de Machaut
> Metr: 32 sts. aaabaaab bbbcbbbc, etc.; octosyllabic except fourth lines have 4 syllables.
> MSS: A B D E G M Vg   Eds: 3 22

Chaucer uses ll. 1–8 of this poem in *Book of the Duchess*, ll. 16–21.

111. f.37a   Rondel

> Inc: Se vo courroux me dure longuement
> Refr: Je ne puis pas avoir longue duree
> Auth: Guillaume de Machaut
> Metr: 8 ll. ABaAabAB; decasyllabics.
> MSS: A B D G M Vg   Eds: 3 22

Machaut has another rondel in the *Louange* with the same first lines.

112. 37a   Complainte

> Inc: Mon cuer mamour ma dame souveraine
> Auth: Guillaume de Machaut
> Metr: 12 sts. aaabaaabbbbabbba; decasyllabics except fourth lines have 4 syllables.
> MSS: A B D E G M Vg   Eds: 3 22

The first sixteen lines form an acrostic MARGUERITE/PIERRE, referring to Pierre of Cyprus, who was in England in 1363 promoting his crusade, and probably Marguerite of Flanders.

113. f.38c   Rondel

> Inc: Je ne pourroye en servant desservir
> Refr: Ce quamours veult dame que je vous serve
> Auth: Guillaume de Machaut
> Metr: 8 ll. ABaAabAB; decasyllabics.
> MSS: A B D E G Vg   Eds: 3 22

114. f.38c   Rondel

> Inc: Mercy vous pri ma doulce dame chiere
> Refr: Qua moy ne soit par vous joye encherie
> Auth: Guillaume de Machaut

Metr: 8 ll. ABaAabAB; decasyllabics.
MSS: A B C E G M Vg   Eds: 3 7 16

This poem appears among Machaut's rondeaux set to music.

115. f.38d   Balade

Inc: Amours me fait desirer
Refr: Que je laye sans rouver
Auth: Guillaume de Machaut
Metr: 3 sts. $a_7a_4b_7a_4a_4b_7b_7b_4a_7b_7b_4A_7$
MSS: A B E G M Vg   Eds: 3 7 8 16 22 23

Appears both in *Louange* and among ballades set to music.

116. f.38d   Rondel

Inc: Quant jay lespart
Refr: De vo regart/dame donnour/Son doulz espart/en moy espart/toute doucour
Auth: Guillaume de Machaut
Metr: 24 ll. AABAABaab, etc.; four-syllable lines.
MSS: A B C E G M Vg   Eds: 3 7 16

Appears among Machaut's rondeaux set to music.

117. f.39a   Rondel

Inc: Comment puet on mieulx ses maulz dire
Refr: A dame qui congnoist honnour
     Et com laime de vraye amour
Auth: Guillaume de Machaut
Metr: 13 ll. ABBabABBabbABB; octosyllabics.
MSS: A B G M Vg   Eds: 3 7 16

Except for line length, this rondeau has the same versification as Chaucer's rondeaux in *Parliament of Fowls* and 'Merciles Beaute.'

118. f.39a   Balade

Inc: Trop me seroit grief chose a soustenir
Refr: Tant pour sonnour com pour la paix de mi
Auth: Guillaume de Machaut
Metr: 3 sts. ababbcC; decasyllabics.
MSS: A B C D E G H M Vg   Eds: 3 22

119. f.39b   Rondel

This poem is identical to No. 81.

120. f.39b   Lay

Inc: Pour ce quen puist mieulx retraire
Auth: Guillaume de Machaut
Metr: 240 ll. in lay form of 24 sts. matched in pairs. Complex rhymes with many short lines.
MSS: A B C E G M Vg   Ed: 3

121. f.40d   Virelay

Inc: Fin cuer tresdoulz a mon vueil
Refr: Font en vous leur droit sejour, etc.
Metr: 33 ll. ABBABbabaabbab, etc; seven-syllable lines.

122. f.41a   Balade

Inc: Espris damours nuit et jour me complains
Refr: Traire il mest grief mais ne men puis retraire
Metr: 3 sts. ababbcC; decasyllabics.
MS: We   Ed: 9

This ballade has 'retrograde' rhymes, with the rhyme syllables repeated at beginning of next lines.

123. f.41b   Virelay

Inc: Doulz regart par subtil atrait
Refr: Au cuer ma si feru et trait, etc.
Metr: 37 ll. AABBAccdccdaabba, etc; octosyllabics.

124. 41c   Rondel

Inc: Revien espoir confort aie party
Refr: Car pitez sest en ma dame endormy
Metr: 8 ll. ABaAabAB; decasyllabics.
MSS: Cam Tr Str Ut   Ed: 1

Appears in Cam and Ut set to music (forms double rondeau with no. 125).

125. 41d   Rondel

Inc: Espoir me faut a mon plus grant besoin
Refr: Com plus me voit en peril plus seslongne
Metr: 8 ll. ABaAabAB
MSS: Cam Tr Str Ut   Ed: 1

Appears (with No. 124) in Cam and Ut set to music.

126. f.41d   Virelay

Inc: Par un tout seul escondire
Refr: De bouche et non du cuer fait, etc.
Metr: 28 ll. ABBAbabaabba, etc.; seven-syllable lines.

127. f.42a   Balade

Inc: Un chastel scay es droiz fiez de lempire
Refr: Cilz chasteaulz est la perilleuse garde
Metr: 3 sts. ababbcC; decasyllabics.
Ed: 9

The narrative of this ballade, parallel to the *Roman de la Rose*, presents the narrator entering the castle of Venus in defiance of a 'dame de raison.'

128. f.42a   Virelay

Inc: Vostre oeil par fine doucour

Refr: Mont mis en plaisant labour, etc.
Metr: 53 ll. AABBAccdccdaabba, etc., 7-syllable lines.

129. f.42c   Balade

Inc: Beaute flourist et jeunesce verdoye
Refr: Celle que dieux et nature ot si chier
Metr: 3 sts. ababbcC; decasyllabics.
Ed: 9

130. 42d   Virelay

Inc: Sans faire tort a nullui
Refr: Puis je bien amer et doy, etc.
Metr: 40 ll. ABBAbabaabba, etc.; 7-syllable lines.

131. 43a   Virelay

Inc: Biaute bonte et doucour
Refr: Faiticite sans folour, etc.
Metr: 47 ll. AABBAcdcdaabba, etc.; 7-syllable lines.

132. f.43b   Balade

Inc: Larriereban de mortele doulour
Refr: Qui par longtemps ma tenu compaignie
Metr: 3 sts. ababbcC
Eds: 5 9

133. 43c   Virelay

Inc: Je me doing a vous ligement
Refr: Ne je nay dautre amour cure, etc.
Metr: 40 ll. ABABcdcdabab, etc.; octosyllabics.

134. 43d   Balade

Inc: Quiconques se complaigne de fortune perverse
Refr: Qui ma rendu ladvis et fait dun fol .j. sage
Auth: Attributed to Eustache Deschamps
Metr: 3 sts. ababbcC; 12-syllable lines.
MS: DeB   Ed: 14

Few *formes fixes* lyrics are composed of alexandrine lines as this one is. It is probably
by Deschamps.

135. f.44a   Virelay

Inc: Onques narcisus en la clere fontaine
Refr: Ne se mira si perilleusement, etc.
Metr: 28 ll. ABABcdcdabab, etc.; decasyllabics.

136. f.44b   Balade

Inc: Se lucresse la tresvaillant rommaine
Refr: A dalida jhezabel et thays

103

Auth: Oton de Granson
Metr: 3 sts. ababccdD; decasyllabic except fifth lines have 7 syllables.
MS: GrA   Ed: 13

Following Machaut in attacking slanderers, Granson brings forward many literary examples.

137. f.44c   Lay

Inc: Amours se plus demandoie
Expl: Explicit le lay du paradis damours
Auth: Guillaume de Machaut
Metr: 198 ll. 24 sts. matched in pairs; complex rhymes; many short lines.
MSS: A B C E G J K M Vg; Paris, BN f.fr. 7220   Eds: 3 18

This lay is an important source of Antigone's song in *Troilus and Criseyde* II 827–75. As is not uncommon with *formes fixes* lyrics, a lady is the narrator here.

138. f.46a   Virelay

Inc: A toy doulz amis seulement me complains
Refr: Et descuevre celeement mes dolens plains, etc.
Metr: 66 ll.; AABAABcccdcccdaabaab, etc.; 8, 10, 11, and 12 syllable lines.

139. f.46c   Virelay

Inc: A poy que mon cuer ne fent
Refr: Tant suis dolent, etc.
Metr: 73 ll.; AABBAABcccdcccdaabbaab, etc.; 7 and 4 syllable lines.

140. f.47a   Virelay

Inc: Avec ce que ne puis plaire
Refr: A ma dame debonnaire, etc.
Metr: 47 ll.; AABBAABbbabbbaaabbaab, etc.; 7 and 5 syllable lines.

141. f.47b   Virelay

Inc: Mon tresdoulz cuer et ma tresdouce amour
Refr: Mon bien ma joye et mon tresdoulz desir
Metr: 33 ll. ABBABababababbab, etc; decasyllabics.

142. f.47c   Balade

Inc: Amis mon cuer et toute ma pensee
Refr: Vous ameray tous les jours de ma vie
Auth: Guillaume de Machaut
Metr: 3 sts. ababbcC; decasyllabics.
MSS: A B D E M Vg   Eds: 3 18 22

143. f.47d   Virelay

Inc: Nest merveille se je change coulour
Refr: Et se sempre ades de jour en jour, etc.
Metr: 36 ll. AABBAcdcdaabba, etc.; decasyllabics.

144. f.48a   Virelay

Inc: Tresdoulz et loyaulz amis
Refr: Cuer et parfaite penser, etc.
Metr: 60 ll. ABABBAccdccdababba, etc.; 7-syllable lines.
MS: PR   Eds: 1 21

Set to music in PR.

145. f.48b   [Rondel]

Inc: Puis quen oubli sui de vous doulz amis
Refr: Vie amoureuse et joye a dieu comment
Auth: Guillaume de Machaut
Metr: 8 ll. ABaAabAB; decasyllabics.
MSS: A E G M   Eds: 3 7 16

Appears in Machaut collections among rondeaux set to music.

146. f.48c   Balade

Inc: En lonneur de ma doulce amour
Refr: Mais sil leur plaist il me plaist bien aussi
Auth: Guillaume de Machaut
Metr: 3 sts. ababccdD; decasyllabic except fifth lines have seven syll-
ables.
MSS: A B D E G M Vg   Eds: 3 22

147. f.48c   Balade

Inc: Honte paour doubtance de meffaire
Refr: Qui de sonnour veult faire bonne garde
Auth: Guillaume de Machaut
Metr: 3 sts. ababccdD; decasyllabic except fifth lines have 7 syllables.
MSS: A B D G J M Vg DeB Fl Tr We   Eds: 3 7 14 16 22

As its appearance in several standard MS anthologies testifies, this ballade was very
popular. It offers words of advice to ladies concerning cautious and moral behavior
in affairs of love. It is set to music in several MSS.

148. f.48d   Rondel

Inc: Helas pourquoy se demente et complaint
Refr: Mon cuer dolent de sa dure douleur
Metr: 8 ll. ABaAabAB; decasyllabics.
Auth: Guillaume de Machaut
MSS: A B C E G M Vg   Eds: 3 7 16

Appears in MSS among Machaut's rondeaux set to music.

149. f.49a   Chanson [Royal]

Inc: Joie plaisance et doulce nourreture
Auth: Guillaume de Machaut
Metr: 5 sts. $a_{10}b_{10}a_{10}b_{10}b_6c_8c_8d_8d_5$; envoy, cdd.
MSS: A B C E F J K M Pep PM Vg   Eds: 4 7 16

This and the next poem are from Machaut's long *dit, Remede de Fortune.* The fact
that most of his poems preceding these in Penn come from the *Louange* and most
that follow from the lyrics set to music and the *Voir Dit* suggests that the anthologist

was drawing from a Machaut collection like MS E, made for the Duke of Berry. See II.A above.

150. f.49b   Virelay

Inc: Dame a vous sans retollir
Refr: Doing cuer pensee desir, etc.
Auth: Guillaume de Machaut
Metr: 67 ll. AABBAABaabaabaabbaab; 4 and 7 syllable lines.
MSS: A B C E F J K M Pep PM Vg   Eds: 4 7 16

Lyrics like this one and the preceding, which are intercalated in *Remede de Fortune*, are set to music in several MSS.

151. f.49d   Balade

Inc: Une vipere ou cuer ma dame maint
Refr: Cil troy mont mort et elle que diex gart
Auth: Guillaume de Machaut
Metr: 3 sts. ababccdD; decasyllabic except fifth lines have 7 syllables.
MSS: A B D E G M We   Eds: 3 7 16 22

This poem is found both in *Louange* and among ballades set to music. The lady has a viper in her heart, a scorpion in her mouth, and a basilisk in her eye, yet the lover invokes God's protection on her.

152. f.49d   Balade

Inc: Nen fait nen dit nen pensee
Refr: Tant com je vivray
Auth: Guillaume de Machaut
Metr: 3 sts. $a_7b_5a_7b_5b_5a_7B_5$
MSS: A B C E G M Vg   Eds: 3 7 16

Found in MSS among ballades set to music.

153. f.50a   Balade

Inc: Je puis trop bien ma dame comparer
Refr: Quades la pry et riens ne me respont
Auth: Guillaume de Machaut
Metr: 3 sts. ababccdD; decasyllabic except fifth lines have 7 syllables.
MSS: A B D E G M Vg   Eds: 3 5 7 16 17 22

Found both in *Louange* and among ballades set to music.

154. f.50b   Balade

Inc: Riches damour et mendians damie
Refr: Quant ma dame me het et je laour
Auth: Guillaume de Machaut
Metr: 3 sts. ababbcC; decasyllabics.
MSS: A B C E G M Vg   Eds: 3 7 16 17

Found in MSS among ballades set to music.

155. f.50c   Balade

Inc: Douls amis oy mon complaint
Refr: Quant tes cuers en moy ne maint

Auth: Guillaume de Machaut
Metr: 3 sts. $a_7a_4a_3b_7a_7a_4a_3b_7b_4b_3a_7b_4b_3A_7$
MSS: A B C E G M Vg   Eds: 3 7 16 18 23

Found in MSS among ballades set to music.

156. f.50d   Balade

Inc: Le desconfort de martire amoureux
Refr: En desirant vostre doulce mercy
Metr: 3 sts. ababbcC; decasyllabics.
Ed. 9

157. f.51a   Balade

Inc: Ceulz dient qui ont ame
Refr: Pour ce nameray plus
Auth: Attributed to Guillaume de Machaut
Metr: 3 sts. ababbcbC; seven-syllable lines.
MS: J   Ed: 3

158. f.51b   Balade

Inc: Se je me plain je nen puis mais
Refr: Ma dame ma congie donne
Auth: Guillaume de Machaut
Metr: 3 sts. ababccdD; decasyllabics.
MSS: A B C E G M Vg   Eds: 3 7 16

Appears in MSS among Machaut's ballades set to music.

159. f.51c   [Balade]

Inc: Dame plaisant de beaute souveraine
Refr: A vous mottry fin cuer gay bonne foy
Metr: 3 sts. ababbcbC; decasyllabics (see below).
Ed: 9

The metrics of this poem are remarkable. Each line divides in three to form vertically three poems rhyming ababbcbC. See Mudge, p. 176.

160. f.51c   Balade

Inc: Phiton le merveilleux serpent
Refr: Quant a ma dame mercy quier
Auth: Guillaume de Maschaut
Metr: 3 sts. ababbcbC; octosyllabics.
MSS: A E G J M Tr   Eds: 3 7 16 23

Appears among Machaut's ballades set to music.

161. f.52a   Rondel

Inc: Dame se vous navez aperceu
Refr: Que je vous aim de cuer sans decevoir
      Essayes le si le sarrez de voir
Auth: Guillaume de Machaut
Metr: 13 ll. ABBabABbabbABB; decasyllabics.
MSS: A B C E G M Vg   Eds: 3 7 12 16

Appears in MSS among Machaut's rondeaux set to music and in *Voir Dit*.

162. f.52a   Balade

> Inc: Esperance qui masseure
> Refr: Que jaim dame satens mercy
> Auth: Guillaume de Machaut
> Metr: 3 sts. ababbcC; octosyllabics.
> MSS: A B C E G M Vg   Eds: 3 7 16

Appears among Machaut's ballades set to music.

163. f52b   Rondel

> Inc: Quant ma dame les mauls damer maprent
> Repr: Elle me puet aussi les biens aprendre
> Auth: Guillaume de Machaut
> Metr: 8 ll. ABaAabAB; decasyllablics.
> MSS: A E G M   Eds: 3 7 16

Appears among Machaut's rondeaux set to music.

164. f.52c   Balade

> Inc: De fortune me doy plaindre et loer
> Refr: Dame qui fust si tres bien assenee
> Auth: Guillaume de Machaut
> Metr: 3 sts. ababccdD; decasyllabics except 7-syllable fifth lines.
> MSS: A B C D E G M Vg Ch PR Str Tr   Eds: 3 5 7 16 22

This popular ballade, in which a lady laments the change in her fortunes in love, appears in MSS both in the *Louange* and among the ballades set to music. A second ballade in MS PR inverts the incipit and refrain of this poem.

165. 52c   Balade

> Inc: Dame de moy bien amee
> Refr: Que lun de nous deux ait congie
> Metr: 3 sts. ababbcbC; octosyllabics.
> Ed: 9

This poem presents an interesting variation. The lover asks the lady to choose between him and his rival.

166. f.52d   Balade

> Inc: Se quanquamours puet donner a ami
> Refr: Contre le bien et la joye que jay
> Auth: Guillaume de Machaut
> Metr: 3 sts. ababccdD; decasyllabics except fifth lines have 7 syllables.
> MSS: A B C E G M Vg We   Eds: 3 7 16

Appears among Machaut's ballades set to music.

167. f.53a   Lay

> Inc: Ne scay comment commencier
> Expl: Explicit le lay de limage
> Auth: Guillaume de Machaut
> Metr: 224 ll. lay form; 24 sts. in pairs, each with differing metrics.

MSS: A B C E G M Vg   Eds: 3 7 16

Set to music in some MSS.

168. f.54d   [Balade]

Inc: Beaute qui toutes autres pere
Refr: Mont a ce mis que pour amer mourray
Auth: Guillaume de Machaut
Metr: 3 sts. ababccdD; decasyllabics except fifth lines have 7 syllables.
MSS: A B C E G M Vg   Eds: 3 7 16 17

Appears among Machaut's ballades set to music.

169. f.54d   Balade

Inc: Sans cuer men vois doulent et esplourez
Refr: En lieu du cuer dame quil vous demeure
Auth: Guillaume de Machaut
Metr: 3 sts. ababccdD; decasyllabics, except fifth lines have 7 syllables.
MSS: A B C E G J M Vg   Eds: 3 7 16

This and the following two ballades have the same form and same refrain, and they
are set to the same music (Triple ballade).

170. f.55a   Balade

Inc: Amis dolens mas et desconfortez
Refr: En lieu du cuer dame qui vous demeure
Auth: Guillaume de Machaut
Metr: 3 sts. ababccdD; decasyllabics except fifth lines have 7 syllables.
MSS: A B C E G J M Vg   Eds: 3 7 16

See note to No. 169.

171. f.55b   Balade

Inc: Dame par vous me sens reconfortez
Refr: En lieu du cuer dame quil vous demeure
Auth: Guillaume de Machaut
Metr: 3 sts. ababccdD; decasyllabics except fifth lines have 7 syllables.
MSS: A B C E G J M Vg   Eds: 3 7 16

See note to No. 169.

172. f.55c   Demi Lay

Inc: Ma chiere dame a vous mon cuer envoy
Auth: Guillaume de Machaut
Metr: 3 sts. aaabaaabbbbabbba; decasyllabic except fourth lines have 4
syllables.
MSS: E G   Eds: 3 7 16

The metrics do not conform to any of the *formes fixes*. Machaut uses the same stanza
in several complaints. Appears with music in two MSS.

173. f.56a   [Balade]

Inc: Gais et jolis lies chantans et joyeux
Refr: Tout pour lespoir que jay de lui veoir

Auth: Guillaume de Machaut
Metr: 3 sts. ababbcC; decasyllabics.
MSS: A B E G M Vg Mo PR We   Eds: 2 3 7 16 22

Appears in MSS among ballades set to music and in *Louange*.

174. f.56a   Balade

Inc: De triste cuer faire joyeusement
Refr: Triste dolent qui larmes de sang pleure
Auth: Guillaume de Machaut
Metr: 3 sts. ababbcC; decasyllabics.
MSS: A B E G M Vg DeB   Eds: 3 7 14 16

Chaucer's *Complaint of Mars*, ll. 155–59, shows important correspondences to this
rhyme royal ballade, which appears in *Louange*, among ballades set to music, and in
Voir Dit. The two poems which follow have the same form and refrain, and are set
to the same music (Triple ballade).

175. f.56b   Balade

Inc: Quant vrais amans aime amoureusement
Refr: Triste dolent qui larmes de sang pleure
Auth: Guillaume de Machaut
Metr: 3 sts. ababbcC; decasyllabics.
MSS: A B E G M Vg   Eds: 3 7 16

See note to No. 174.

176. f.56c   Balade

Inc: Certes je dy et senquier jugement
Refr: Triste doulent qui larmes de sang pleure
Auth: Guillaume de Machaut
Metr: 3 sts. ababbcC; decasyllabics.
MSS: A B E G M Vg   Eds: 3 7 16

See note to No. 174.

177. f.56d   Rondel

Inc: Tant doulcement me sens emprisonnez
Refr: Quonques amant not si doulce prison
Auth: Guillaume de Machaut
Metr: 8 ll. ABaAabAB; decasyllabics.
MSS: A B C E G M Pe Vg Tr   Eds: 3 7 16

Appears in MSS among Machaut's rondeaux set to music.

178. f.56d   Balade

Inc: Quant theseus hercules et jason
Refr: Je voy assez puis que je voy ma dame
Auth: Guillaume de Machaut
Metr: 3 sts. ababccdD; decasyllabics except fifth lines have 7 syllables.
MSS: A B E F G M Vg Ch DeB PR   Eds: 3 7 12 14 16 17 21 23

This and the next ballade have the same form, refrain, and music (Double ballade).
They appear in the *Voir Dit*, as well as among ballades set to music, and were
obviously quite popular.

179. f.57a   Balade

Inc: Ne quier veoir la beaute dabsalon
Refr: Je voy assez puis que je voy ma dame
Metr: 3 sts. ababccdD; decasyllabics except fifth lines have 7 syllables.
MSS: A B E F G M PM Vg Ch DeB PR
Eds: 3 7 12 14 16 17 21 23

See note to No. 178. Froissart's Ballade VI imitates this poem, having a similar incipit and identical refrain. The list of nonpareils, cited for beauty, strength, wisdom, etc., bears comparison with the list of Chaucer's *Book of the Duchess*, ll. 1056–72.

180. f.57b   Balade

Inc: Flour de beaute de tresdoulce oudour plaine
Refr: Je nen puis mais se je men desconforte
Metr: 3 sts. ababbcbC; decasyllabics.
Ed: 9

181. f.57b   Rondel

Inc: Se vous nestes pour mon guerredon nee
Refr: Dame mar vy vo doulz regart riant
Auth: Guillaume de Machaut
Metr: 8 ll. ABaAabAB; decasyllabics.
MSS: A B C E G M PM Vg Ca Fl Mo Pg   Eds: 2 3 5 7 16

Appears among rondeaux set to music in MSS.

182. f.57c   Lay

Inc: Sonques douloureusement
Expl: Explicit un lay (other MSS: 'Le Lay de comfort')
Auth: Guillaume de Machaut
Metr: 272 ll. with 24 sts. in matched pairs of differing metrics.
MSS: A B E G J K M Vg   Eds: 3 7 16

Chaucer uses ll. 10–13 of this lay in *Book of the Duchess*, ll. 693–96. The lay is set to music in some MSS.

183. f.59c   Balade

Inc: Mercy ou mort ay long temps desire
Refr: Si prie amours que mort ou amez soye
Metr: 3 sts. ababbcC; decasyllabics.
MS: PR   Ed: 5 9 21

184. f.59c   Balade

Inc: He doulz regart pourquoy plantas lamour
Refr: Maudit de dieu soit qui en toy se fie
Auth: Ascribed to Eustache Deschamps
Metr: 3 sts. ababbcC; decasyllabics.
MSS: DeB   Eds: 5 14

The poem is probably not by Deschamps.

185. f.59d   Virelay baladé

Inc: Combien qua moy lointeine
Refr: Soyes dame donnour, etc.
Auth: Guillaume de Machaut
Metr: 40 ll. ABABabababab, etc.; 6 syllable lines.
MSS: A B C E G M Vg   Eds: 1 3 7 16

The adjective 'baladé' in the virelay rubrics indicates that the poem is set to music (though it is not in Penn, of course, which has only the words of the poems).

186. f.60a   Virelay baladé

Inc: Puis que ma doulour agree
Refr: A la debonnaire nee, etc.
Auth: Guillaume de Machaut
Metr: 66 ll. AAABAAABbbabbaaaabaaab, etc.; 5 and 7 syllable lines.
MSS: A B C E G M Vg   Eds: 3 7 16

Appears in MSS among Machaut's virelays set to music.

187. f.60c   Balade

Inc: Par un gracieux samblant
Refr: Dame que vous mavez fait
Metr: 3 sts. ababbcC; 7-syllable lines.
Eds: 1 9

188. f.60d   Balade

Inc: Jugiez amans et ouez ma dolour
Refr: Elle me het et est mon anemie
Auth: Attributed to both Guillaume de Machaut and Eustache Deschamps
Metr: 3 sts. ababccdD; decasyllabics.
MSS: J DeB   Eds: 1 3 5 14

Probably by neither Machaut nor Deschamps.

189. f.61a   Balade

Inc: Se lancelot paris genievre helaine
Refr: Doulce dame pour vostre amour avoir
Metr: 3 sts. ababccdD; decasyllabics except fifth lines have 7 syllables.
MS: We   Ed: 9

This is an effective poem in which the lover says that he is burning up with thirst beside the fountain, which is too high for him. The incipit is like the double ballade of Grimace which follows in Penn. A ballade in MS Ch, edited in 5, has a similar incipit.

190. f.61b   Balade

Inc: Se zephirus phebus et leur lignie
Refr: Se devant moy ma dame ne veoye
Auth: Grimace
Metr: 3 sts. ababbcC; decasyllabics.
MSS: Ch Pl   Eds: 1 9

This and the following ballade have the same metrical form, refrain, and music (Double ballade).

191. f.61b   Balade

Inc: Se jupiter qui par grant melodie
Refr: Se devant moy ma dame ne veoye
Auth: Grimace
Metr: 3 sts. ababbcC; decasyllabics.
MSS: Ch PI   Ed: 1 9

See note to No. 190.

192. f.61c   Virelay baladé

Inc: Se mesdisans en accort
Refr: Sont pour moy grever a tort, etc.
Auth: Guillaume de Machaut
Metr: 54 ll. AABBBAccbccbaabbba, etc.; 5, 6, and 7 syllable lines.
MSS: A B C E G M Vg   Eds: 3 7 16 18

Appears in MSS among virelays set to music.

193. f.62a   Virelay baladé

Inc: Cest force faire le vueil
Refr: Tuit mi desir, etc.
Auth: Guillaume de Machaut
Metr: 54 ll. ABBABAbbcbbcabbaba, etc.; 7 and 4 syllable lines.
MSS: A B C E G M Vg   Eds: 3 7 16

Appears among verelays set to music.

194. f.62b   Rondel

Inc: Dame doulcement attrait
Refr: Avez tout le cuer de mi
Metr: ABaAabAB; 7-syllable lines.

195. f.62c   Rondel

Inc: Douls amis de cuer parfait
Refr: Ligement a vous mottry
Metr: 8 ll. ABaAabAB; 7-syllable lines.

196. f.62c   Le Lay de plour

Inc: Malgre fortune et son tour
Auth: Guillaume de Machaut
Metr: 272 ll. in lay form; 24 sts. in pairs, each pair with differing metrics.
MSS: A G M   Eds: 3 7 16

Appears in MSS with music.

197. f.64c   Rondel

Inc: Doulz cuers gentilz plain de toute franchise
Refr: A vous amer me sui abandonnez
Metr: 8 ll. ABaAabAB; decasyllabics.

198. f.64d   Virelay baladé

> Ind: Cent mil fois esbaye
> Refr: Plus dolente et plus courroucie, etc.
> Auth: Guillaume de Machaut
> Metr: 67 ll. AABBAABccdccdaabbaab, etc.
> MSS: A E F PM   Ed: 12

Appears in *Voir Dit*. Between No. 198 and No. 227 in Penn fourteen lyrics are from the *Voir Dit*, a late, long pseudo-autobiographical poem.

199. f.£5a   Rondel

> Inc: Tant com je seray vivant
> Refr: Vous seray loyal amie
> Auth: Guillaume de Machaut
> Metr: 8 ll. ABaAabAB; 7-syllable lines.
> MSS: A E F PM   Ed: 12

Appears in *Voir Dit*.

200. f.65a   Balade

> Inc: Se par fortune la lasse et la desvee
> Refr: Car cuer donnez ne se doit retolir
> Auth: Guillaume de Machaut
> Metr: 3 sts. ababbcC; decasyllabics.
> MSS: A E F PM   Eds: 7 12 16

Appears in *Voir Dit*.

201. f.65b   Virelay baladé

> Inc: Dame vostre doulz viaire
> Refr: Debonnaire, etc.
> Auth: Guillaume de Machaut
> Metr: 60 ll. AABAABbbabbaaabaab, etc.; 7 and 4 syllable lines.
> MSS: A B C E G M Vg   Eds: 1 3 7 16

Appears in MSS among Machaut's virelays set to music.

202. f.65c   Rondel

> Inc: Soyes liez et menez joye
> Refr: Amis car amours men proye
> Auth: Nicole de Margival
> Metr: 16 ll. AABBAaAAaabbAABB; octosyllabics
> MSS: Pg Str; Paris, BN f.fr.22432; St. Petersburg, Hermitage, 53.
> Eds: 5 19

This is ll. 2515–26 of *Le Dit de la Panthère d'Amours*, by Nicole de Margival, which has some significant correspondence in structure to Chaucer's *House of Fame*. See above II E.

203. f.65d   Balade

> Inc: Ne soyes en nul esmay
> Refr: Vostre jusques au mourir
> Auth: Guillaume de Machaut
> Metr: 3 sts. ababbcC; ostosyllabics.

MSS: A E F PM   Ed: 12 18

Appears in *Voir Dit*.

204. f.66a   Virelay baladé

Inc: Onques si bonne journee
Refr: Ne fu adjournee, etc.
Auth: Guillaume de Machaut
Metr: 60 ll. AABAABbbabbaaabaab, etc.; lines of 5 and 7 syllables.
MSS: A E F PM   Ed: 12

Appears in *Voir Dit*.

205. f.66b   Rondel

Inc: Esperance qui en mon cuer sembat
Refr: Sentir me fait damer la doulce vie
Metr: 8 ll. ABaAabAB; decasyllabics.

206. f.66c   Virelay baladé

Inc: Helas et comment aroye
Refr: Bien ne joye, etc.
Auth: Guillaume de Machaut
Metr: 60 ll. AABAABccbccbaabaab, etc.; lines of 3 and 7 syllables.
MSS: A B C E G M Vg   Eds: 3 7 16

Appears in MSS among Machaut's virelays set to music.

207. f.66d   Rondel

Inc: Autre de vous jamais ne quier amer
Refr: Tresdoulz amis a qui jay donne mamour
Auth: Guillaume de Machaut
Metr: 8 ll. ABaAabAB; decasyllabics.
MSS: A E F PM   Eds: 12 18

Appears in *Voir Dit*.

208. f.66d   Balade

Inc: Le plus grant bien qui me viengne damer
Refr: Quassez rouve qui se va complaignant
Auth: Guillaume de Machaut
Metr: 3 sts. ababccdD; decasyllabic except fifth lines have 7 syllables.
MSS: A B C D E F G J M PM Vg

Appears in MSS in *Louange* and *Voir Dit*.

209. f.67a   Rondel

Inc: Tresdouls amis quant je vous voy
Refr: Tout faites mon cuer resjoir
Auth: Guillaume de Machaut
Metr: 8 ll. ABaAabAB; octosyllabics.
MSS: A E F PM   Eds: 14 18

Appears in *Voir Dit*.

115

210. f.67b   Virelay baladé

Inc: Dieux beaute doulceur nature
Refr: Mirent bien tout leur faiture, etc.
Auth: Guillaume de Machaut
Metr: 74 ll. AAABAAABbbcbbcaaabaaab, etc.; lines of 7 and 5 syll-
ables.
MSS: A B C E G M Vg   Ed: 3 7 16

Appears in MSS among virelays set to music.

211. f.67c   Balade

Inc: Le bien de vous qui en beaute florist
Refr: Et voz regars maintient mon cuer en joye
Auth: Guillaume de Machaut
Metr: 3 sts. ababbcC; decasyllabics.
MSS: A B C D E F G J M Vg   Eds: 3 8 14 22

Appears in *Louange* and *Voir Dit*.

212. f.67d   Virelay baladé

Inc: Se damer me repentoye ne faignoye
Refr: Trop feroye contre mi, etc.
Auth: Guillaume de Machaut
Metr: 48 ll. AABAABbabaaabaab, etc.; lines of 3 and 7 syllables.
MSS: A B C E G M Vg   Eds: 3 7 16 18

Appears in MSS among Machaut's virelays set to music.

213. f.68a   Virelay baladé

Inc: En mon cuer a un descort
Refr: Qui si fort le point et mort, etc.
Auth: Guillaume de Machaut
Metr: 67 ll.; AABBAABbbabbaaabbaab, etc.; lines of 4 and 7 syllables.
MSS: A B E G M Vg   Eds: 3 7 16

Appears among Machaut's virelays set to music.

214. f.68c   Rondel

Inc: Ma dame doulce et debonnaire
Refr: Flour de valour, etc.
Metr: 16 ll. ABBAbaABBabbaABBA; lines 8 and 4 syllables.

215. f.68c   Virelay baladé

Inc: Mors sui se je ne vous voy
Refr: Dame donnour, etc.
Auth: Guillaume de Machaut
Metr: 67 ll. ABBBAABaabaababbbaab, etc.
MSS: A B C E G M Vg   Eds: 3 7 16

Appears among Machaut's virelays set to music.

216. f.68*a   Rondel

Inc: Amis doulz amer sans retraire

Refr: Et sans foulour, etc.
Metr: 16 ll. ABBAbaABabbaABBA; lines of 8 and 4 syllables.

Two folios in succession in Penn are numbered 68.

217. f.68*a   Virelay baladé

Inc: Plus dure que un dyamant
Refr: Ne que pierre daymant
Auth: Guillaume de Machaut
Metr: 67 ll. AABBAABbbabbaaabbaab, etc.
MSS: A B G M Vg   Eds: 3 7 16 23

Appears among Machaut's virelays set to music.

218. f.68*c   Rondel

Inc: Doulce pite que or tesveille
Refr: Ou cuer de la tendre flour, etc.
Metr: 16 ll. ABBAbaAABabbaABBA; 7 syllable lines.

219. f.68*c   Virelay baladé

Inc: Dame mon cuer emportez
Refr: Dont tant sui desconfortez, etc.
Auth: Guillaume de Machaut
Metr: 67 ll.; AABBAABbbabbaaabbaab, etc.; lines of 7 and 4 syllables.
MSS: A B E G M Vg   Eds: 3 7 16

Appears among Machaut's virelays set to music.

220. f.69a   Virelay baladé

Inc: Tres belle et bonne mi oeil
Refr: Joyeuse pasteure, etc.
Auth: Guillaume de Machaut
Metr: 60 ll. ABBAABbbabbaabbaab, etc.; lines of 7 and 5 syllables.
MSS: A B C D E G M   Eds: 3 7 16 22

Appears among Machaut's virelays set to music and in *Louange*.

221. f.69c   Virelay baladé

Inc: Doulce plaisant et debonnaire
Refr: Onques ne vy vo doulz viaire, etc.
Metr: 53 ll. AABBAccaccaaabba, etc.; octosyllabics.

222. f.69d   Virelay baladé

Inc: Cilz a bien fole pensee
Refr: Qui me cuide a ce mener, etc.
Auth: Guillaume de Machaut
Metr: 46 ll. ABABccdccdabab, etc.; lines of 7 syllables.
MSS: A B C E F G M PM Vg   Eds: 3 12 18

Appears in *Voir Dit* and among Machaut's virelays set to music, but no music is extant.

223. 70b [Balade]

Inc: Nes quon pourroit les estoilles nombrer
Refr: Le grant desir que jay de vous veoir
Auth: Guillaume de Machaut
Metr: 3 sts. ababbcC; decasyllabics.
MSS: A B D E F G M PM Vg   Eds: 3 7 8 12 16 22

Appears in *Louange*, *Voir Dit*, and among ballades set to music.

224. f.70b Rondel

Inc: Toute belle bonne cointe et jolie
Refr: Bieneureux seroit ce mest advis
Metr: 11 ll. ABBaAabbABB; decasyllabics.

225. f.70c Virelay baladé

Inc: Loeil qui est le droit archier
Refr: Plus doulce que nest doulcour, etc.
Auth: Guillaume de Machaut
Metr: 67 ll. AABBAABbbabbaaabbaab, etc.; lines of 7 and 4 syllables.
MSS: A B E F G M PM Vg   Eds: 3 12

Appears in *Voir Dit* and among virelays set to music, but no music is extant.

226. 70d Virelay baladé

Inc: Plus belle que le beau jour
Refr: Plus doulce que nest doulcour, etc.
Auth: Guillaume de Machaut
Metr: 67 ll. AABBAABbbabbaaabbaab, etc.; lines of 7 and 4 syllables.
MSS: A B E F G M PM Vg   Eds: 3 12

Appears in *Voir Dit* and among virelays set to music, but no music is extant.

227. f.71b Virelay baladé

Inc: Je ne me puis saouler
Refr: De penser dymaginer, etc.
Auth: Guillaume de Machaut
Metr: 67 ll. AABBAABbbabbaaabbaab, etc.
MSS: A B E F G M PM Vg   Eds: 3 12

Appears in *Voir Dit* and among virelays set to music, but no music is extant.

228. f.71c Balade

Inc: Je vous mercy des belles la plus belle
Refr: Ma belle dame et ma loyal amie
Auth: Oton de Granson
Metr: 3 sts. ababbccdcD; decasyllabics.
MS: GrA   Ed: 13

229. f.71d Balade

Inc: De la douleur que mon triste cuer sent
Refr: Celle qui est des plus belle la flour
Metr: 3 sts. ababbcC; envoy, abbcC; decasyllabics.
Ed: 9

Before this ballade, the only ballade in Penn which has an envoy is No. 20. After No. 229 and 230, there are no other ballades with envoys until No. 267. Envoys came to be added to ballades commonly in the last quarter of the fourteenth century.

230. f.72a   Balade

       Inc: Vray dieu damours plaise toy secourir
       Refr: Se ainsi est que jaye perdu la belle
       Metr: 3 sts. ababbacaC; envoy, acacaC; decasyllabics.
       Ed: 9

231. f.72b   Balade

       Inc: Povre perdue dolente et esgaree
       Refr: Comme la plus maleureuse du monde
       Metr: 3 sts. ababcdcD; decasyllabics.
       Ed: 9

232. f.72c   Balade

       Inc: Gente belle corps fait par compasseure
       Refr: Se ne mestes de remede prochaine
       Metr: 3 sts. ababbcbC; decasyllabics.
       Ed: 9

233. f.72d   Balade

       Inc: Puis quainsi est que ne puis nullement
       Refr: Que vostre amour sans cesser me fait traire
       Metr: 3 sts. ababbcC; decasyllabics.
       Ed: 9

234. f.73a   Lay

       Inc: Au commencier du mois de may
       Metr: 218 ll. in lay form of 24 stanzas in matched pairs of differing metrics. Some stanzas seem defective.

235. f.74c   Chanson royal / Ch

       Inc: Entre les biens que creature humainne
       Metr: 5 sts. ababbccdede; envoy, de; decasyllabics.
       Ed: 24 (above)

This is the first of the 'Ch' poems. The last is No. 276.

236. f.75a   Balade

       Inc: Mort je me plain de qui de toy
       Refr: Car tout prendray soit feble ou fort
       Auth: Attributed to Eustache Deschamps
       Metr: 3 sts. ababbcC; octosyllabics.
       MS: DeB   Ed: 14

This interesting ballade is a dialogue between Death and the lover whose lady Death has taken. Most lines include statement / question with response. It is probably by Deschamps.

237. f.75a   Balade/Ch

Inc: Oncques doulour ne fu plus angoisseuse
Refr: Que fons et fris comme au feu fait la cire
Metr: 3 sts. ababbccdcD; decasyllabics.
Eds: 9 24

238. f.75b   Balade

Inc: Samours plaisoit ses tresors defermer
Refr: Quant ma dame me donna nom damy
Metr: 3 sts. ababbcC; decasyllabics.
Ed: 9 24 (I Appendix above)

This ballade has the same refrain as the 'Ch' poem which follows. The versification differs.

239. f.75c   Balade/Ch

Inc: Je cuide et croy que tous les joieux jours
Refr: Quant ma dame me donna nom dami
Metr: ababbccdcD; decasyllabics.
Ed: 9 24

240. f.75d   Chancon royal/Ch

Inc: Aux dames joie et aux amans plaisance
Metr: 5 sts. ababbccdd; envoy d; decasyllabics.
Ed: 9 24

241. f.76a   Balade/Ch

Inc: Fauls apyus pires que lichaon
Refr: Jone mamas et vieille mas guerpie
Metr. 3 sts. ababbccddedE; decasyllabics.
Eds: 9 24

The refrain and content of No. 35 is quite like the refrain and content of this ballade.

242. f.76b   Balade/Ch

Inc: Nous qui sommes trois filles a phebus
Refr: Viel Saturnus et sa dure lignie
Metr: 3 sts. ababbccdcD; decasyllabics.
Eds: 9 24

243. f.76c   Complainte amoureuse

Inc: Ma doulce amour ma dame souverainne
Metr: 120 ll. aaaabbbbbc, etc.; decasyllabics except fifth lines 4 syllables.

This complaint has numerous similarities to Machaut's Complaint VI (Penn No. 112), written by Machaut for Pierre of Cyprus. Coming as it does amidst the 'Ch' poems, it is perhaps a work of 'Ch'.

244. f.77c   Balade / Ch

Inc: Plus a destroit et en plus forte tour
Refr: Ne me fait brief en pluie dor muer
Metr: 3 sts. ababbccdcD; decasyllabics.
Eds: 9 24

245. f.77d   Balade / Ch

Inc: Humble hester courtoise gracieuse
Refr: Pourrist en terre et je remains sans dame
Metr: 3 sts. ababbccdcD; decasyllabics.
Eds: 9 24

246. f.77d   Balade

Inc: Des yeulx du cuer plorant moult tendrement
Refr: Du lit de plours doulereux ou je gis
Metr: 3 sts. ababbcbC; decasyllabics.
Ed: 9

This lover's complaint is answered by the lady who speaks in the following ballade.

247. f.78a   Balade

Inc: Se tu seuffres pour moy painne et martire
Refr: En ce doulx mois que chascuns se jolie
Metr: 3 sts. ababbcC; decasyllabics.
Ed: 9

See note to No. 246.

248. f.78b   Balade

Inc: Maintes gens sont qui dune grant valee
Refr: Mais quant lui plaist jus labat en peu deure
Metr: 3 sts. ababbcbC; decasyllabics.
Ed: 9

249. f.78c   Chancon royal / Ch

Inc: Pour le hauls biens amoureux anoncier
Metr: 5 sts. ababbccdcd; envoy, cd; decasyllabics.
Ed: 24

250. f.78d   Balade

Inc: Cuidiez vous je vous en pry
Refr: Adieu adieu le varlet
Metr: 3 sts. ababbcbC; 7 syllable lines.
Ed: 9

The lady scornfully sends the jangling 'varlet' away.

251. f.79a   Balade

Inc: Or ne scay je tant de service faire
Refr: Plus mescondit plus la vueil tenir chiere

Auth: Oton de Granson
Metr: 3 sts. ababbcbC; decasyllabics.
MS: GrA   Ed: 13

From No. 252 to 264, there are at least eight poems of Granson mixed in with some 'Ch' and anonymous works. The Granson poems appear elsewhere only in MS GrA.

252. f.79b   Balade

Inc: A medee me puis bien comparer
Refr: Ainsi le fit cuer plain de faussete
Auth: Oton de Granson
Metr: 3 sts. ababbcbC; decasyllabics.
MS: GrA   Ed: 13

253. f.79c   Balade

Inc: Or nay je mais que dolour et tristesce
Refr: Se je men dueil nul ne men doit blasmer
Auth: Oton de Granson
Metr: 3 sts. ababbcC; decasyllabics.
MS: GrA   Ed: 13

254. f.79d   Balade

Inc: Vous qui voulez loppinion contraire
Refr: Desloiaute en lamoureuse vie
Auth: Oton de Granson
Metr: 3 sts. ababbcbC; decasyllabics.
MS: GrA   Ed: 13

255. f.79d   Balade

Inc: He dieux amis qui vous meut a ce faire
Refr: Ce nest pas fait de loial amoureux
Metr: 3 sts. ababbcbC; decasyllabics.
Ed: 9

In its position among Granson poems and its use of versification favored by Granson, one may well suspect that this ballade is his.

256. f.80a   Balade

Inc: Se mon cuer font en larmes et en plours
Refr: Pour mercy garder de ma dame le fort
Auth: Oton de Granson
Metr: 3 sts. ababbcbC; decasyllabics.
MS: GrA   Ed: 13

257. f.80b   Balade

Inc: Dames de pris qui amez vostre honnour
Refr: Ilz ne tendent le plus qua decevoir
Metr: 3 sts. ababbcbC; decasyllabics.

As with No. 255, and for the same reasons, one might attribute this poem to Granson.

258. f.80c   Balade

　　　　Inc: Qui veult entrer en lamoureux servage
　　　　Refr: Ainsi puet il don damours desservir
　　　　Auth: Oton de Granson
　　　　Metr: 3 sts. ababbcbcB; decasyllabics.
　　　　MS: GrA   Ed: 13

259. f.80d   Balade

　　　　Inc: Cest bonne foy de deux cuers amoureux
　　　　Refr: Dangier ny puet ne aussi jalousie
　　　　Metr: 3 sts. ababbcbC; decasyllabics.
　　　　Ed: 9

As with No. 255 and No. 257 there are good reasons for ascribing this ballade to Granson.

260. f.80d   Rondel/Ch

　　　　Inc: Qui veult faire sacrefice a venus
　　　　Refr: Ou temple dont elle est droite deesse
　　　　Metr: 8 ll. ABaAabAB; decasyllabics.
　　　　Ed: 24

This is the only rondeau of 'Ch' and the only rondeau in Penn between No. 224 and 277.

261. f.81a   Balade

　　　　Inc: Ne doy je bien malebouche hair
　　　　Refr: Sa ma cause perdoit sa bonne fame
　　　　Auth: Oton de Granson
　　　　Metr: 3 sts. ababbcbC; decasyllabics.
　　　　MS: GrA   Ed: 13

262. 81a   Balade

　　　　Inc: Qui en amours quiert avoir son desir
　　　　Refr: Qui ce ne scet amours le fait savoir
　　　　Metr: 3 sts. ababbcbC; decasyllabics.
　　　　Ed: 9

263. f.81b   Chancon royal/Ch

　　　　Inc: Venez veoir qua fait pymalion
　　　　Metr: 5 sts. ababccddede; envoy, dede; decasyllabics.
　　　　Ed: 24

As I have noted, this poem is inferior to the other 'Ch' works.

264. f.81d   Balade

　　　　Inc: Amis pensez de loyaument amer
　　　　Refr: Vous nen povez tousdiz que miex valour
　　　　Auth: Oton de Granson
　　　　Metr: 3 sts. ababbcbC; decasyllabics.
　　　　MS: GrA   Ed: 13

265. f.81d   Balade

Inc: A ce printemps que je sens revenir
Refr: Pour les faire trestous crever denvie
Metr: 3 sts. ababbcbC; decasyllabics.
Ed: 9

266. f.82a   Complainte amoureuse

Inc: Doulx ami que jaim loyalment
Metr: 124 ll. aaabaaabbbbcbbbccccd, etc.; octosyllabic except fourth
lines have 4 syllables.

267. f.83a   Balade

Inc: A dieu a dieu jeunesse noble flour
Refr: Car on ne puet passer par autre voie
Metr: 3 sts. ababbcbC; envoy, bcbC; decasyllabics.
Ed: 9

This is only the fourth ballade in Penn with an envoy. The next is No. 279.

268. f.83b   Balade

Inc: Voir ne vous puis helas ce poise moy
Refr: On y verroit lemprainte de mes yeulx
Metr: 3 sts. ababbccdcD; decasyllabics.
Ed: 9

269. f.83b   Balade

Inc: Pluseur se sont repenti
Refr: Et qui ne se veult brusler
     Si se traie en sux
Auth: Guillaume de Machaut
Metr: 3 sts. $a_7b_5a_7b_5b_7c_7d_5c_7D_5$
MSS: A B C D E G H J K M Vg   Eds: 3 22

270. f.83c   Balade

Inc: Langue poignant aspre amere et ague
Refr: Je le feray mourir de dueil ou taire
Auth: Guillaume de Machaut
Metr: 3 sts. ababbcC; decasyllabics.
MSS: A B C D E G J M Vg We   Eds: 3 22

In the *Book of the Duchess*, ll. 639–41, and the Merchant's Tale, ll. 2058–62,
Chaucer ascribes to Fortune description which this ballade uses to attack slanderers.

271. f.83d   Balade

Inc: Amis si parfaitement
Refr: E sil est autre qui bee
     A mamour il y fauldra
Auth: Guillaume de Machaut
Metr: 3 sts. $a_7b_5a_7b_5c_7d_7c_7d_7$

MSS: A B C D E F G J M PM Vg   Eds: 3 12 18 22

Appears both in *Louange* and *Voir Dit*.

272. f.84a   Virelay

Inc: Le doulx songe que lautre nuit songoie
Refr: Cestoit veir ma doulce dame chiere, etc.
Metr: 53 ll. ABBAAcddcddabbaa, etc.; decasyllabics.

The lines are unusually long for the virelay form.

273. f.84b   Balade / Ch

Inc: Mort le vy dire et si ny avoit ame
Refr: A son ame soit dieu misericors
Metr: 3 sts. ababbccdcD; decasyllabics.
Eds: 9 24

274. f.84c   Balade / Ch

Inc: Oez le plains du martir amoureux
Refr: Il vit sans joye et languist en mourant
Metr: 3 sts. ababbccdcD; decasyllabics.
Eds: 9 24

275. f.84d   Balade / Ch

Inc: De ce que jay de ma douleur confort
Refr: Grace a ma dame et loenge a amours
Metr: 3 sts. ababbcbC; decasyllabics.
Eds: 9 24

276. f.85a   Balade / Ch

Inc: Qui partiroit mon cuer en .ij. parmi
Refr: Sourse donnour et riviere de joie
Metr: 3 sts. ababbccdcD; decasyllabics.
Eds: 9 24

277. f.85b   Rondel

Inc: Mon tresdoulx cuer et ma seule pensee
Refr: A mon povoir tousjours vous serviray
Metr: 16 ll. ABBAabABabbaABBA; decasyllabics.

From No. 277 to the end of Penn (No. 310), there are no poems of known authorship, nor any clues (like 'Ch' may be). From No. 272 to the end, the texts in Penn are unique; i.e., are found in no other extant MSS.

278. f.85b   Virelay

Inc: Vous ne savez le martire
Refr: Que mon povre cuer si tire, etc.
Metr: 37 ll. AABBAccbccbaabba, etc.; lines of 7 syllables.

279. f.85c   Balade

        Inc: Pourquoy virent onques mes yeulx
        Refr: Puis quil lui plaist il me souffist
        Metr: 3 sts. ababbccdcD; envoy, bccdcD; decasyllabics.

Seven of the seventeen balades from No. 279 to the end have envoys. Only four before No. 279 have them.

280. f.86a   Rondel

        Inc: Puis quainsi est quamours mont estrangee
        Refr: De tous les biens que souloye avoir, etc.
        Metr: 16 ll. ABBAabABabbaABBA; decasyllabics.

281. f.86a   Balade

        Inc: Vous me povez faire vivre ou mourir
        Refr: Vostre doulx cuer si si vueille acorder
        Metr: 3 sts. ababbccdcD; envoy, cdcD; decasyllabics.
        Ed: 9

This balade and the preceding rondel are among the numerous lyrics in Penn in which a lady is the speaker. Here she promises to obey his every command.

282. f.86b   Rondel

        Inc: Mes yeulx mon cuer et ma pensee
        Refr: Par leur pourchas mont mis a mort, etc.
        Metr: 16 ll. ABBAabABabbaABBA; octosyllabics.

283. f.86c   Chancon royal

        Inc: Mere je sui assez povre de sens
        Metr: 7 sts. ababbccddee; envoy, ddee; decasyllabics.

This extended chant royal is a dialogue between a mother and daughter about love; each speaks a stanza at a time.

284. f.87a   Rondel

        Inc: Se vo doulx cuer ne mue sa pensee
        Refr: Et que par lui grace me soie donnee, etc.
        Metr: 21 ll. AABBAaabAABaabbaAABBA; decasyllabics.

285. f.87b   Virelay

        Inc: Bien doy chanter liement
        Refr: Et plus amoureusement, etc.
        Metr: 27 ll. AABBAABbbabbaaabbaab, etc.

The form is either defective or represents a late experiment.

286. f.87c   Balade

        Inc: Tout droit au temps que doivent les doulcours
        Refr: Lomme qui pert a poinne se puet taire
        Metr: 3 sts. ababbcC; decasyllabics.
        Ed: 9

287. f.87c   Rondel

        Inc: Par ma foy je nen puis mais
        Refr: Se suis en dolente painne, etc.
        Metr: 16 ll. ABBAabABbabbaABBA; 7 syllable lines.

288. f.87d   Balade

        Inc: Puis que je voy que ma belle maistresse
        Refr: Que par nulle autre joye me fust donnee
        Metr: 3 sts. ababbccddeefeF; envoy, ababbccfcF; decasyllabics.
        Ed: 9

The stanza is unusually long.

289. f.88a   Rondel

        Inc: Quant je ne puis vers vous mercy trouver
        Refr: De la doulour qui par vous mest donnee, etc.
        Metr: 16 ll. ABBAbaABbabbaABBA; decasyllabics.

290. f.88b   Balade

        Inc: Mon seul vouloir mon seul bien ma maistresse
        Refr: Que dautre amer aye jamais vouloir
        Metr: 3 sts. ababbccdeD; decasyllabics.
        Ed: 9

291. f.88c   Rondel

        Inc: Certes belle se je devoye
        Refr: Tousjours languir sans grace avoir, etc.
        Metr: 16 ll. ABBAbaABbabbaABBA; octosyllabics.

292. f.88d   Balade

        Inc: Jamais nul jour ne pourroye desservir
        Refr: Tout vostre sui quelque part que je soye
        Metr: 3 sts. ababbcaC; decasyllabics.
        Ed: 9

293. f.88d   Rondel

        Inc: Vo grant beaute qui mon cuer tient joyeux
        Refr: Ma vraie amour et quanque je desire, etc.
        Metr: 16 ll. ABBAbaABbabbaABBA; decasyllabics.

294. f.89a   Balade

        Inc: Puis quamours mont donne tel hardement
        Refr: Qui sur toutes en avez le povoir
        Metr: 3 sts. ababbcC; decasyllabics.
        Ed: 9

295. f.89b   Rondel

        Inc: Je ris des yeulx et mon povre cuer pleure

Refr: Et si ny puis avoir aucun secours, etc.
Metr: 16 ll. ABBAbaABabbaABBA; decasyllabics.

296. f.89b   Balade

Inc: Se je navoye plus de biens
Refr: Il pourroit bien avenir mais
Metr: 3 sts. ababbcbC; envoy, bcbC; octosyllabics.
Ed: 9

297. f.89c   Rondel

Inc: Tant my fait mal le partir de ma dame
Refr: Que je nay jeu bien nesbatement, etc.
Metr: 16 ll. ABBAabABabbaABBA; decasyllabics.

298. f.89d   [Balade]

Inc: A vous le dy courroux dueil et tristrece
Refr: Helas amours je ne le cuidoye mie
Metr: 3 sts. ababbcbC; envoy, bbcbC; decasyllabics.
Ed: 9

299. f.90a   Rondel

Inc: Plus quautre belle se je sui loing de vous
Refr: Et que veir ne vous puisse a mon gre, etc.
Metr: 16 ll. ABBAabABabbaABBA; decasyllabics.

300. f.90a   Balade

Inc: Ce seroit fort que je peusse avoyr joye
Refr: Car pour plus belle jamais homs ne mourra
Metr: 3 sts. ababbcbC; decasyllabics.
Ed: 9

301. f.90b   Balade

Inc: Oyez mes plains tous loyaulx amoureux
Refr: Mamour est morte et ma joye si fine
Metr: 3 sts. ababbcbC (first st. defective); decasyllabics.
Ed: 9

302. f.90c   Balade

Inc: Belle qui de toutes bontez
Refr: Mais quil vous plaise a moy amer
Metr: 3 sts. ababbccdcD; decasyllabics.
Ed: 9

303. f.90d   Balade

Inc: Des que premiers vo beaute regarday
Refr: Faites de moy tout ce quil vous plaira
Metr: 3 sts. ababccdcD; envoy, cdcD; decasyllabics.
Ed: 9

304. f.91a   Rondel

Inc: Tant quil vous plaira
Refr: Ma belle maistresse, etc.
Metr: 16 ll. ABBAbaABabbaABBA; lines of 5 syllables.

305. f.91b   Balade [for Pastourelle]

Inc: A leure que bergiers leur pain
Refr: A faire de roses chappeaulx
Metr: 5 sts. ababbccdcD; envoy, cdcD; octosyllabics.

This is the only pastourelle after the twelve which come at the beginning of Penn.

306. f.91c   Rondel

Inc: Ma belle amour ma joyeuse esperance
Refr: Tout quanque jaim et que je vueil servir
Metr: 16 ll. ABBAbaABabbaABBA; decasyllabics.

307. f.91d   Balade

Inc: Entre mon cuer et mes yeulx grant descort
Refr: Faire mon cuer a mes yeulx accorder
Metr: 3 sts. ababbccdcD; decasyllabics.
Ed: 9

308. f.92a   Balade

Inc: Tu as tant fait par ta tresbonne attente
Refr: Quant a cela certes je my oppose
Metr: 3 sts. ababbcC; decasyllabics.
Ed: 9

309. f.92b   Balade

Inc: En mon dormant mavint la nuit passee
Refr: Se je savoye quainsi deusse songier
Metr: 3 sts. ababbcdcD; envoy, dcdcD; decasyllabics.
Ed: 9

310. f.92c   Balade

Inc: Aucunes gens dient quen bien amer
Refr: Que vrays amans ne puet sans jalousie
Metr: 3 sts. ababbcC; decasyllabics.
Ed: 9

This poem turns about a major commonplace of Amour, which holds that true lovers cannot avoid jealousy, and it provides a reasonably apt conclusion for the collection. Eight folios were left blank after it, however, which suggests that more poems could have been envisaged.

Index of First Lines of Poems Edited Herein

Notes

I. The Poems of 'Ch'—Introduction pp. 1–8

1 The 'Ch' initials were inserted in a different, neat hand after the manuscript had been written; no space had been allowed for them. Possibilities for the significance of the initials, besides indicating authorship, are that they stand for either 'chanson' or 'chant,' referring to a poetic form or to the presence of accompanying music. However, there seems no way of accounting for the ten balades and the rondel as 'chants' or 'chansons,' and most of the poems are not of a form customarily set to music. Only the rondel and the short ballade (with eight-line stanzas) would be likely to have musical settings. At the same time, numerous other poems in Penn have known settings. See also the discussion by Charles Mudge, *The Pennsylvania Chansonnier, A Critical Edition of Ninety-five Anonymous Ballades from the Fourteenth Century*, University of Indiana doctoral diss. (Ann Arbor: University Microfilms, 1972), p. 6. Mudge thinks 'Ch' may signal authorship, but he hazards no guesses as to the author.

2 The poetic careers of Alain Chartier, Christine de Pisan, and Charles d'Orleans all postdate composition of the manuscript.

3 The various factors suggesting mid-century authorship and an English locale are presented in this introduction below, and especially in Part II of this study.

4 The chant royal and the ballade have separate origins, but Deschamps, and other poets near the same time, mixed the types by employing refrains in the chants and adding envoys to the ballades.

5 See Daniel Poirion, *Le Poète et le prince* (Paris: Presses Universitaires de France, 1965), p. 372.

6 Chants royaux were frequently composed for the *puys*. Five of six of Froissart's chants and related serventois were 'crowned' at different *puys* in northern France. See Rob Roy McGregor, Jr., ed., *The Lyric Poems of Jehan Froissart*, Univ. of North Carolina Studies in the Romance Langs, and Lits., No. 143 (Chapel Hill: Univ. of North Carolina Press, 1975), pp. 194–204.

'Ch' of course could have been a resident of England and still written the envoy of 'The Lady's Perfection.' He could have composed it for a *puy* in France while on a visit; he could have written it for an English *puy*; or he could have addressed the envoy to the 'Prince of the Puy' simply as a matter of convention.

7 Ten of eleven lines in stanza one begin with 'Venez veoir'; eight in stanza two with 'Avisez bien'; four in stanza three with 'Ymaginez'; and 'C'est' is used seven times to begin sentences in stanza four. We might compare this heavy-handed employment of anaphora with the tactful use of 'La est'/'La sont' in three consecutive lines in stanza three of #I.

8 Some translations in stanzas two, four, and five of #I, while representing possible solutions, are more tentative than most translations herein.

9 In general the text which the manuscript provides, though far from perfect, is quite good. In the 'Ch' poems there is only one point (IX, l. 31) where the reading is clearly wrong and no reasonable emendation presents itself.

II. Chaucer and University of Pennsylvania MS French 15 (Penn) pp. 47–77

1 Professor Jeanne Krochalis, who is quite familiar with Penn, states that the date of the script 'could definitely be before 1400,' though she does not rule out placing it a little later. She identifies the scribes as French, as does A. I. Doyle of Durham University, England. As the latter notes, the French origin of the scribes does not exclude its having been written in England. On the basis of an inspection of the microfilm, Dr Karen Gould concludes that there were at least two scribes. She identifies a change in scribes very near the center of the MS, between folios 48v and 49r; text no. 149, the first of the

two poems by Machaut from *Remede de Fortune*, begins f.49. I am indebted to the forenamed scholars, as well as Profs. Carter Revard and Linda Voigts, for their generous and expert advice concerning the date and provenance of the manuscript.

2 Charles R. Mudge, *The Pennsylvania Chansonnier, a Critical Edition of Ninety-five Anonymous Ballades from the Fourteenth Century*, Univ. of Indiana diss. (Ann Arbor: University Microfilms, 1972), pp. 10–11. There are two not insuperable objections to Mudge's hypothesis. The first is that the motto of Bavaria was placed on the MS long after its making and Isabelle's death in 1434; one must postulate, then, that the connection of the codex with Isabel and Bavaria was maintained or understood after she died—not at all impossible. The second objection is that Granson's poems to Isabel probably were composed much before she came to Paris and married Charles in 1385. Nevertheless, if they were not written for her in the first place, they would have been readily adaptable to her when Granson met her after 1385; lyrics that he perhaps composed for Isabel of York could be presented a second time to Isabelle of Bavaria. For the identification of Granson's Isabel as Isabel of York, see Haldeen Braddy, *Chaucer and the French Poet Granson* (Baton Rouge: Louisiana State Univ. Press, 1947), pp. 73–80. In arguing that the Isabel of the poems was Isabelle of Bavaria, and her alone, Arthur Piaget, *Oton de Grandson: sa vie et ses poésies*, Société d'Histoire de la Suisse Romande, 3ᵉ série (Lausanne: Payot, 1941), pp. 156–64, ignores the evidence for the dates of composition.

3 There are four other lyrics in Penn that have been attributed to Machaut (nos 36, 37, 157, 188), but they are not in the full collections that the poet himself supervised and are probably not his.

4 From the *Louange* in this part of Penn are nos 72, 81–115, 118, 119, 142, 146; from the lyrics set to music nos 116, 117, 120, 137, 145, 147, 148.

5 *Remede de Fortune* lyrics are 149 and 150.

6 From the lyrics set to music are 151–55, 158, 160–64, 166–79, 181, 182, 185, 186, 192, 193, 196, 201, 206, 210, 212, 213, 215, 217, 219, 220, 222, 223, 225–27; lyrics found only in *Voir Dit* are 198–200, 203, 204, 207–09, 211.

7 Nos 269–71. In the arrangement of Machaut poems in Penn, these probably entered as an afterthought.

8 See the chart of contents of the Machaut collections in F. Ludwig, *Guillaume de Machaut: Musikalische Werke*, I (Leipzig, 1926), 43*. J, K, B, and Vg alone agree with E in having the *Louange* preceding the long *dits*, but they lack the text of *Voir Dit*. Vg and B agree with E also in including the complaints among the *Louange* texts, as the exemplar for Penn evidently did; the later Machaut collections segregated the complaints. Yet it is to be noted that Penn contains two Machaut texts (nos 72 and 172) that are elsewhere found only in the later collections. This complicates the picture.

9 *Les Cents Ballades*, ed. Gaston Raynaud, Société des Anciens Textes Français (Paris: Firmin–Didot, 1905), p. 213. The Duke's poem echoes Chaucer's 'Merciles Beaute.'

10 For Chaucer's uses of Machaut's lyrics, with references to the important earlier scholarship, see James I. Wimsatt, 'Guillaume de Machaut and Chaucer's Love Lyrics,' *Medium Aevum*, 47 (1978), 66–87; and 'Chaucer, Fortune, and Machaut's "Il m'est avis,"' in Edward Vasta and Zacharias Thundy, eds., *Chaucerian Problems and Perspectives* (Notre Dame, Ind.: Notre Dame Univ. Press, 1979), pp. 119–31. The poems included in Penn that Chaucer used (identified by the text numbers in V.-F. Chichmaref, ed., *Guillaume de Machaut: Poésies lyriques*, 2 vols. [Paris: Champion, 1908]) are *Louange* CXC, CCXXIII, CCLXII; Complaintes I, VI; Lays IX, XVII; Balades notées XXXII, XXXVIII, XLIII.

11 See James I. Wimsatt, ed., *The Marguerite Poetry of Guillaume de Machaut*, Univ. of North Carolina Studies in the Romance Langs. and Lits., no. 87 (Chapel Hill: Univ. of North Carolina Press, 1970), pp. 41–59.

12 Granson's poems in Penn are nos 18, 20–34, 136, 228, 251–54, 256, 258, 261, 264.

13 Braddy, pp. 57–61, 64–66, sees the influence going the other way; but see James

I. Wimsatt, *Chaucer and the French Love Poets*, University of North Carolina Studies in Comp. Lit., No. 43 (Chapel Hill: Univ. of North Carolina Press, 1968), pp. 143–46.

14 Mudge, pp. 12–13. Mudge had planned to treat in full the relationship between these works of Chaucer and Granson, but he evidently was not able to do so before he died.

15 Ed. Auguste Scheler (Louvain: J. Lefever, 1882).

16 Ed. E. Pognon, 'Balades mythographiques de Jean de le Mote, Philippe de Vitri, Jean Campion,' *Humanisme et Renaissance*, 5 (1938), 409–410, 414–15.

17 In his edition of the unpublished ballades of Penn, Charles Mudge transcribes the pair, with no attempt to edit, in an appendix of texts that 'appear to be considerably corrupt and full of insoluble problems,' pp. 150, 153–54.

18 Pognon, hampered by the bad text, does not note the allusion to Dante.

19 While Dante states that Minos winds his tail around himself as many times as the steps ('gradi,' V. 12) that he is sending the soul down, it is not clear at this point whether the starting point is Minos' position in the second circle, or the top of the Inferno. If the former, then seven times around as Philippe specifies will take the soul to circle nine with the traitors. Later, Guido da Montefeltro makes clear that the latter is meant (XXVII.124–26).

20 *Metamorphoses* V.253–59. In Philippe's frame of reference, to 'make Pegasus fly' (l. 26), I take it, is to write effective poetry.

21 See A. Coville, 'Philippe de Vitri: notes biographiques,' *Romania*, 59 (1933), 544; and Pognon, 'Balades mythographiques,' pp. 400, 415 (n. to l. 7).

22 Jean de le Mote, *Le Parfait du Paon*, ed. Richard J. Carey, Univ. of North Carolina Studies in the Romance Langs. and Lits., no. 118 (Chapel Hill: Univ. of North Carolina Press, 1972). Pognon, 'Balades mythographiques,' p. 391, evades the evidence of Campion's reference to Jean's *Parfait* (Appendix B, ll. 2–3) and much else in dating the Philippe–Jean exchange between 1328 and 1339. Little supports such a date.

23 Ed. E. Pognon, 'Du nouveau sur Philippe de Vitry et ses amis,' *Humanisme et Renaissance*, 6 1939), pp. 50–52. The attack on the unnamed poet appears in Motetus, ll. 15–20, and Triplum, ll. 1–34.

24 Brian Trowell, 'A Fourteenth-Century Ceremonial Motet and Its Composer,' *Acta Musicologica*, 29 (1957), 65–75.

25 Trowell, p. 67.

26 Below are the passages in Jean's ballade (placed second) which are parallel, and thus are presumed sources, to parts of Deschamps' two ballades (placed first and third). The parallel words and phrases are in italics. Deschamps ballades are found in *Oeuvres completes d'Eustache Deschamps*, ed. le marquis de Queux de Saint-Hilaire and Gaston Raynaud, Société des anciens textes français, 11 vols. (Paris: Firmin–Didot, 1878–1904), I, #124; II, #285.

Deschamps to Machaut: *O* fleur des fleurs de toute melodie,
Tresdoulz *maistres* qui tant fustes adrois,
O Guillaume, *mondains dieux d'armonie*,
Apres voz faiz, qui obtendra le chois
Sur tous faiseurs? Certes, ne le congnoys.
Vo noms sera precieuse relique,
Car l'en plourra en France et en Artois
La mort Machaut, le noble rethorique.

La fons Circe et *la fonteine Helie*
Dont vous estiez le ruissel et les dois . . .

Jean to Philippe: *O* Victriens, *mondains dieu d'armonie*,
Filz Musicans et per a Orpheus,
Supernasor de *la fontaine Helye*,
Doctores vrays, *en* ce *pratique Anglus*,

Plus clers veans et plus agus qu'Argus,
Angles en chant, cesse en toy le lyon.

. . . .

T'a fait brasser buvrage a trop de lie
Sur moy qui ay de toy fait Zephirus,
Car en *la fons Ciree* est tes escus . . .

Deschamps to Chaucer: O Socrates plains de philosophie,
Seneque en meurs et *Anglux en pratique*,
Ovides grans en ta poeterie,
Briés en parler, saiges en rethorique,
Aigles treshaulz, qui par ta theorique
Enlumines le regne d'Eneas,
L'Isle au Geans, ceuls de Bruth, et qui as
Semé les fleurs et planté le rosier,
Aux ignorans de la langue pandras,
Grant translateur, noble Geffroy Chaucier.

. . . .

A toy pour ce de *la fontaine Helye* . . .

An incidental matter that the comparison makes clear is that the reading 'fons Circe' in the Deschamps poem to Machaut is incorrect. It should be 'Ciree.'

27 See Antoine Thomas, 'Jean de le Mote, trouvère,' *Histoire Littéraire de la France*, XXXVI (Paris: Imprimerie Nationale, 1926), 70.

28 *Calendar of Patent Rolls, 1338–40*, p. 189.

29 For date of poem, see Schéler, ed., ll. 4572–73.

30 For the relationship between *BD* and *Li Regret Guillaume*, see Constance Rosenthal, 'A Possible Source of Chaucer's *Book of the Duchess—Li Regret de Guillaume* by Jehan de la Mote,' *MLN*, 48 (1933), 511–14; and Wimsatt, *Chaucer and the French Love Poets*, pp. 147–49.

31 For names of Simon and poet, and date of poem, see Carey, ed., ll. 3895–3919.

32 Ed. Sr. M. Aquiline Pety, O. P. (Washington, D.C.: Catholic Univ. of America Press, 1940).

33 *Poésies de Gilles Li Muisis*, ed. Kervyn de Lettenhove, 2 vols. (Louvain: Lefever, 1882), I, 89.

34 See Campion's ballade, Appendix B, ll. 14–16.

35 *Calendar of Patent Rolls*, 1360–64, p. 203; Kervyn de Lettenhove, *Chroniques de Froissart*, I, pt. 1 (Brussels: Devaux, 1870), 76n.

35a After this book went to press, a recent discovery by Nigel Wilkins came to my attention which documents Jean de le Mote's presence in England after he wrote the two long poems for Simon of Lille. An entry in the controller's book for July 21, 1343 shows le Mote being paid for entertaining King Edward at Eltham. See Wilkins, 'Music and Poetry at Court: England and France in the Late Middle Ages,' *English Court Culture*, Colston Symposium (London: Duckworth, 1983), in press.

36 For Philippe's life and work, see Ernest H. Sanders, 'Vitry, Philippe de,' *The New Grove's Dictionary of Music and Musicians* (London: McMillan, 1980), XX, 22–28; and A. Coville, 'Philippe de Vitri, notes biographiques,' *Histoire Littéraire de la France*, XXXVI (Paris: Imprimerie Nationale, 1925), 520–47.

37 For the friendship of Petrarch and Bersuire with Philippe, see Coville, esp. pp. 531–36.

38 Deschamps, *Oeuvres*, V, #872; VIII, #1474.

39 E. Langlois, ed., *Recueil d'Arts de Seconde Rhétorique* (Paris: Imprimerie Nationale, 1902), p. 12.

40 Gace de la Buigne, *Le Roman des deduis*, ed. Ake Blomquist, Studia Holmiensia, III (Karlshamn: Johanssons, 1951), ll. 6345–56.

41 Two balades which illustrate Jean's somewhat extravagant use of names precede

the exchange between Philippe and Jean in B. N. latin 3343 (*B*). These are edited by Pognon in 'Balades mythographiques,' pp. 407–408.

42 See, e.g., 'Ch', V, 17–21 above; Campion, Appendix B, ll. 1–5; Chaucer, *Anelida and Arcite*, ll. 15–20; *House of Fame*, ll. 519–22; and *Troilus and Criseyde*, III, 1809–11. The various references to 'Ciree,' 'Cirrea' (Cirrha) in their relationships to Dante, *Paradiso* I.36 provide one interesting aspect of this series of references to Apollo and the Muses.

43 MS Paris, Bibliothèque Nationale, fonds français nouv acq. 6221 is described at length in *Oeuvres de Deschamps*, II, xvii–xliv; the editor describes all of the Deschamps MSS in XI, 101–11. Those poems of MS 6221 which are not edited in the body of the *Oeuvres* (vols. I–IX) are edited in 'Pièces attribuables à Deschamps,' *Oeuvres*, X, i–xciv.

44 The use of envoys with ballades became common in the latter part of the fourteenth century among poets who were not musicians; they were never invariably employed. The musical form of the ballade did not accomodate the envoy. Machaut, a musician writing early, did not employ them. Froissart (b. 1335, but active into the fifteenth century) seems never to have added envoys to his ballades, and Granson did but seldom. It was Deschamps who really took to them and no doubt was largely responsible for their vogue.

45 The fourteen ballades of the Penn MS which also appear in MS 6221 are Penn nos. 43, 44, 55, 69, 77, 88, 134, 147, 174, 178, 179, 184, 188, and 236. A fifteenth poem, a rondel used as an illustrative example in the *Art de Dictier* in MS 6221, is Penn no. 105.

46 These are Penn nos. 43, 44, 55, 77, 134, and 236.

47 Though his work has marked differences from Machaut's, Deschamps learned the craft from Machaut and evidently remained very much under his influence. The several ballades he wrote on Machaut's and DuGuesclin's deaths (1377 and 1380) lack envoys; the ballade to Chaucer (around 1385) has one.

48 I am not suggesting that Machaut wrote all of these poems, but only that they were written in imitation of Machaut's work and capture its spirit.

49 Froissart's pastourelles are edited by Rob Roy McGregor, Jr., *The Lyric Poems of Jehan Froissart*, Univ. of North Carolina Studies in the Romance Langs. and Lits., no. 43 (Chapel Hill: Univ. of North Carolina Press, 1975), pp. 151–93.

50 In the *Art de Dictier*, Deschamps, *Oeuvres*, VII, 287, identifies the serventois as an 'ouvrage qui se porte au Puis d'Amours, et que nobles hommes n'ont pas acoustumé de ce faire.' For this reason he gives no examples of the serventois; subsequently, he gives similar short shrift to the pastourelle (VII, 287). The standard form of the pastourelle and the serventois is five stanzas with an envoy. While most of the Middle French five-stanza forms usually had decasyllabic lines, octosyllabics came to be associated with the pastourelle. For an edition of the Penn pastourelle section, with discussion of the development of the Middle French form, see William W. Kibler and James I. Wimsatt, 'The Development of the Pastourelle in the Fourteenth Century: An Edition of Fifteen Poems with an Analysis' (forthcoming).

51 These are poems nos 6 and 7 in the MS. Both involve dialogues between shepherds lamenting recent events. The first makes reference to a number of battles in the Hundred Years War from its beginning to 1359, and the second is probably based on the pillaging in northern France by 'routiers' in 1357 and 1358. The fifteenth poem of the pastourelle section is an allegory involving the black lion of Flanders, the fleur de lis of France, and the leopard of England; it is perhaps the last of the works in time of composition (the later 1360's). This work paints a rather negative picture for England of the current political situation, while the others that deal with political matters are neutral complaints about the ravages of the War.

52 Ed. Henry A. Todd, Société des Anciens Textes Français (Paris: Firmin–Didot, 1883). Margival is a village in the north of France near Soissons; the narrator, l. 48, places himself in Soissons when he has his dream.

53 Albert C. Baugh, 'Chaucer and the *Panthère d'Amours*,' *Brittanica Festschrift für Hermann M. Flasdieck* (Heidelberg: Winter, 1960), pp. 51–61, discusses the scho-

larship on the subject, mainly dismissing previously alleged connections between the *Panthère* and *House of Fame*, but then he brings forward some parallels of his own. I have made my case for its influence in *Chaucer and the French Love Poets*, pp. 58–61.

54 For information on Grimace, see Gilbert Reaney, 'Grimace,' in Friedrich Blume, ed., *Die Musik in Geschichte und Gegenwart*, Bd. 5 (Kassel: Bärenreiter, 1956), cols. 920–22; and Nigel Wilkins, 'The Post-Machaut Generation of Poets,' *Nottingham Medieval Studies*, 12 (1968), 57. Reaney suggests that the name is a pseudonym.

55 For analysis and statistical summary of the lyric and stanza types of much of the corpus of ascribed lyrics in Middle French, see Daniel Poirion, *Le Poète et le prince* (Paris: Presses Universitaires de France, 1968), pp. 303–97.

56 Machaut similarly places a more formally-titled and well-developed Prologue, composed late in his career, at the head of his collected works. In light of the fact that envoys with ballades came into fashion after Granson began writing, the placement of his other ballades with envoys in the later parts of the major Granson collections (i.e., Neuchatel and Paris) suggests a rough chronological ordering. The MSS of Machaut's and Froissart's works have such approximate arrangement.

57 These seven ballades of Granson appear elsewhere only in the Neuchatel MS, while his other poems in Penn appear at least in the Paris and Neuchatel collections. Since none of the ballades unique to Neuchatel have envoys, it is likely that they belong to a group composed earlier than the rest of his works, among which are several ballades with envoy.

58 In MSS and edition, the Granson rondeaux appear mostly as ten-line forms, but in these the scribes and editor have not allowed for or indicated the necessary repetition of the refrain. Thus what is presented as ABBA ab abba should appear as ABBA abAB abba ABBA.

59 Nicole's poem does not have quite the same rhyme scheme as the other sixteen-line rondeaux, but it is close. All of the works essentially double the eight-line form.

60 See Poirion's table, pp. 385–87.

61 See note 2 above.

62 See Braddy, pp. 26–28.

63 See Piaget, pp. 49–51, 75–77, 110–11.

64 Ed. in Amadée Pagès, *La Poésie française en Catalogne du XIIIᵉ siècle à la fin du XVᵉ siècle* (Paris: Didier, 1936).

Appendix A: Granson's Five Ballades   pp. 69–74

1 MSS A, B, and C are the same as GrA, GrB, and GrC listed below in Part III, Key to Abbreviations for Manuscripts. The editions of Piaget, Schirer, and Pagès are numbers 13, 15, and 11 respectively in the Key to Abbreviations for Editions.

2 In A the Five Balades are found on f. 100r–101v (I–III), 113r–v (IV), and 88r–v (V); in B f.75v–77v (I–V); in C. f.414r–415r (I–IV), 411r (V).

3 See Mudge, p. 12.

III. The Contents of Penn
A. The Significance of the Contents of the Manuscript   p. 78

1 The only rivals in interest to Penn among anthologies of fourteenth-century French lyric texts are Paris, Bibliothèque Nationale fonds français nouv. acq. 6221, Westminster Abbey 21, and the two collections which contain *Les Cents Ballades* and lyrics of Granson: B.N.f.fr.2201, and Neuchâtel, Bibl. Arthur Piaget VIII. B.N.6221 is discussed in II D above. The Westminster Abbey MS is a good collection but contains only fifty-six pieces.

2 For Bertoni's inventory, see No. 2 in Key to Editions below, pp. 6–14.

3 For Mudge's list, see Edition No. 9, pp. 244–344.